Our Heritage of Old Roses

Our Heritage
of
OLD ROSES

Judyth A. McLeod

Kangaroo Press

For Keith who has always filled my life
with love and roses.

Cover: 'Fantin Latour' perhaps the greatest of all the Centifolia roses

This edition first published in 1987 by Kangaroo Press Pty Ltd
3 Whitehall Road (P.O. Box 75) Kenthurst NSW 2156
Typeset by G. T. Setters Pty Limited
Printed in Hong Kong by Colorcraft Ltd

ISBN 0-86417-168-4

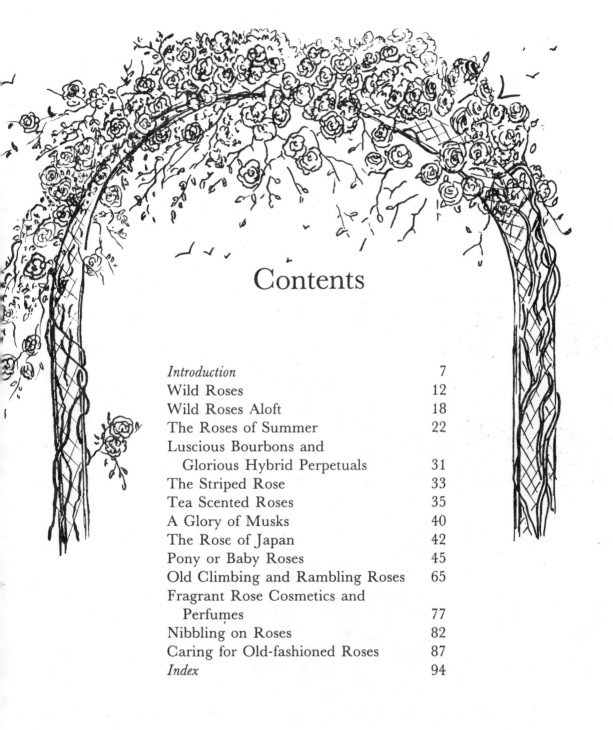

Contents

Introduction

The goosebery, raspberry and roses, all three
With strawberries under them truly agree.

Thomas Tutter (c. 1520–80)

Most of us carry gardens in our hearts. The gardens I lived in as a child are still with me—a tropical garden on volcanic soil looking down onto brilliant sapphire seas, a garden fragrant with frangipani and white ginger flower, brilliant with cascading bougainvillea and oleander, paths lined with huge tropical corals and shells that were an Antipodean equivalent of the garden of 'Mary, Mary quite contrary'. There were big country gardens filled with fragrant spider lilies and massive bushes of old Tea roses, and nodding-headed Noisettes breaking down ancient archways with their burden of blossom.

And then there were Tasmanian family gardens, sheep properties on Tasmania's east coast on which five generations had lived, and the town houses that went with a once comfortable way of life.

I can remember, even in the 1950s, there were shepherds who had been born on these old properties and lived still in charming stone cottages with gardens that might have been photographed for an English calendar, so full were they of hollyhocks and foxgloves, sweet mignonette, heartsease and forget-me-nots, ivy geraniums, perennial poppies, lavender, rosemary, sweet alyssum, grannies bonnets and, cascading everywhere—across the welcoming arch at the entrance, over picket fences, under the eaves, and hedging small orchards and vegetable gardens—old roses.

In the more formal homestead gardens with their wide flagged verandahs and old bricked paths edged with tiles were great hedges of hydrangeas, cherry geraniums, lilies, cottage flowers, and more old roses. At Christmas we would raid huge bushes of holly and pick scarlet rowan berries to decorate the house. The rowan was always planted at the entrance, to carry on an unbroken if dimly remembered tradition from a time when it was said to keep witches from entering.

The trees we climbed into and played in as children are now the subject of serious study by garden historians—an odd fate for a comfortable ancient pear or conifer!

With such a basket of memories it was only too probable that as a professional botanist and ecologist I would, in time, drift toward garden history and restoration, to the field of antique cultivars, and above all to the collection and propagation of the old roses of Australia's colonial past.

Today, in a mountain garden of several acres looking down on the beautiful historic Hawkesbury Valley, we have recreated a patchwork of childhood memories for my husband Keith (a fellow botanist) and myself. Gathered into this sheltered demi-paradise ringed by bellbirds and flourishing in rich basaltic soil are thousands of different old and antique plants. And, as in those childhood gardens, the roses reign supreme. They cascade down embankments, cover arches and pergolas, fill walkways and spill over paths. Gathered together are many hundreds of old Gallicas, Damasks, Albas, Centifolias, Mosses, Bourbons, Portlands, Chinas, Teas, Hybrid Perpetuals, Noisettes, rambler roses and others.

The search for these ancient and lovely old plants, survivors of the centuries, is a never-ending fascination. Marie-Antoinette, Henry VIII and his many wives, Jane Austen, and the Empress Josephine may all be dead but many of the roses that they loved and sniffed with such pleasure are still alive. Old varieties of fruits, roses and the like are living history, and it never ceases to excite me that a rose that grows now in my garden has grown in the gardens of so many others, perhaps for many centuries.

Roses are part of the story of Australia. Wherever pioneers went, roses were to accompany them to new homes agonisingly remote from their countries of origin.

The First Fleet could not have arrived in Australia at a much worse time to begin survival gardens. January in Sydney, on the sandy soils of the harbour, is very hot and dry and it must have been unbelievably difficult for English people used to a gentle climate with adequate rainfall. Yet in 1788 George Worgan, the surgeon on board *Sirius*, was able to describe a ten acre garden successfully sown to supply the table of the Governor. The garden was sited where today's picturesque Sydney Domain stands, on mostly very sandy soils, and the seeds were planted in a season reasonably appropriate for England but not for our burning long summers. Not unexpectedly, George Worgan reported that 'the Plants degenerate in their growth exceedingly'. Nevertheless much survived and in that first year the garden contained many vegetables: broadbeans, peas, turnips, potatoes, yams ('that flourish better than others') and pumpkins. More exotic plants such as ginger, coffee, oranges, lemons, limes, indigo, firs and oaks were also planted. With a climate produced by the overlapping of the northern tropics and southern temperate zone, Sydney was to prove suitable for growing such an extraordinary range of materials, although better soils away from the harbour and salt spray drift would be required to prove it.

How alien this country must have seemed, strange and beautiful and unforgiving. It was possible to survive off the land but it needed the expertise of Australia's first inhabitants to do it. Here were no rich excesses of luscious tropical fruits and thirst quenching coconuts such as Defoe might have conjured up for his adventurous Robinson Crusoe. Here was a bush of exceeding beauty: soft, feathery, honey and fragrance rich but, it seemed almost devoid of edible foliage and fruit. Indeed the medicinal uses of the oil-rich vegetation outweighed its contribution to early larders.

How natural then that those early settlers should have clung to living reminders of a safer home and loved ones left half way round the world. How precious became a rose plant, a honeysuckle, an iris or a lavender.

Roses were among the very early plant imports into Australia. The records of Sir William Macarthur of Camden and Alexander Macleay of Elizabeth Bay House and 'Brownlow Hill', among others, reveal a steady flow of old roses entering the country, accompanying ornamental trees and the more practical fruit, nut and windbreak varieties. Among those early listings were small China roses, Centifolias, Mosses, Damasks and Gallicas. The plant lists for Elizabeth Bay House in the late 1840s included *R. noisette*, *R. banksiae* and *R. bracteata* (Macartney rose). (It also included a very long and sophisticated list of herbs, shrubs and trees, particularly of Chinese origin, such as magnolias, *Prunus* species, rhododendrons, camellias, *Ailanthus*, azaleas, gardenias, lilies, *Holmskioldia*, mourning iris and others.)

The records show such men to have been most generous to fellow gardeners in the colonies and these roses were quickly shared around once they had been propagated by garden staff. Cottages, provided with so much more land than had been available to many in England, and often with higher and happier expectations on the part of their owners, showed neat rows of many vegetables together with fruit trees, vines, the same seed-raised cottage plants we love today—Canterbury bells, hollyhocks, larkspurs, sweet scabious, sweet William, heartsease, sunflower, nasturtium, primrose—and from cuttings, honeysuckles and jasmines of different kinds, lilacs, and roses.

Old graveyards from the early nineteenth century were often marked by some treasured old rose, and they survive and bloom there still. Childrens' graves of which there were so pitifully many to be seen in places like Rookwood, were particularly likely to be marked with some gentle, fragrant, often pale pink rose. The Bourbon 'Souvenir de la Malmaison' and the Tea 'Duchesse de Brabant', together with little China roses, seem to have been favoured in the mid-nineteenth century, although earlier the Gallicas held sway.

The story of the rose in New Zealand closely parallels its introduction into Australia, but what a different reception it received in one of the kindest lands on earth. Whereas Australia is an ancient continent, weathered, worn, harsh of climate, with characteristically low nutrient soils, in New Zealand the soils are, for the most part, rich, loamy and geologically young, and the climate is characterised by mildness and reliable rainfall.

Some of New Zealand's roses came by seed, the sweet briar and the dog rose, others like the little Chinas grew easily from cuttings in pots, while the glories of France, great Centifolias, Mosses, Damasks, Gallicas and others are known to have reached the country packed in moss and sealed in metal tubes. The list of roses that entered New Zealand in its first twenty years of European settlement is an extraordinary and diverse one.

In many ways Australia and New Zealand have become a repository for the great roses of the past. The sunny warmer climate allowed many roses with tender China blood in their veins to survive untended if necessary, while in many parts of Europe considerable cossetting or even glasshouse conditions were needed to bring them through long harsh winters. In cooler areas Gallicas and other old summer-flowering roses survive tangled along broken country fence lines and beside homesteads, and in late spring make gay otherwise lonely and abandoned old pioneers' graveyards and deserted cottages in forgotten towns.

Late in the twentieth century, interest in these living antiques and in the styles of garden they once adorned has reached an unprecedented level. Discriminating gardeners of some years ago, like Gertrude Jekyll, Vita Sackville-West, Constance Spry and Margery Fish in England and Edna Walling in Australia, through their work and writings, encouraged a gardening public, perhaps too preoccupied with being fashionable and contemporary, to value their inheritance from the past. It is certainly not a new thing to value our plant heritage or to appreciate the beauty that our gardening forebears have handed down to us. But these talented gardeners spoke to a relatively small audience and thousands of antique plants that, had they been heirlooms in the form of furniture, jewellery and the like, would have been treasured, were dug out and left to wither on compost heaps. An old chair in an attic may yet survive to be appreciated once more, but not a plant uprooted. The impact of World War I in Europe with its social upheavals and need for self-sufficiency in food production accounted for countless ornamental plant losses, and for incalculable damage to historically valuable gardens.

In the 1950s and 1960s, in a postwar fever of growth and affluence, Australians tore down many glories of their colonial architecture. But the last quarter of a century has seen increasing value placed on nineteenth century and early twentieth century residences that might once have been razed to the ground to make way for modern homes and developments. It has become an absorbing task for many owners of older residences to restore them to their former state, and to fill them with appropriate antiques.

A similar awareness has now developed of the need to extend this process to the outside: to restore the design of the garden in a manner appropriate to the original period, furbishing it with plant materials authentically in use in the nineteenth century, and the furnishings once common to the colonial garden.

Not everyone has the opportunity to restore an old home but many people today wish for a retreat from the pressures and fears of modern life, an escape hatch into a past that, at least from this distance, seems to have been quiet and peaceful and infinitely desirable. The plants of our past form a living link between those days and now. It is remarkable how these fragrant gently coloured old plants transmit a feeling of total restfulness when gathered into a modern garden. Even better, so strong and healthy are these old varieties that the gardener need feel no guilty urge to be up and doing in a garden that is designed and planted to heal and restore.

The plant materials available to the gardener in nineteenth century Australia were a rich and eclectic mixture and can for the most part still be obtained today from specialist nurseries. The old perennials so favoured then were almost universally tough and hardy. Fragrant old world herbs such as rosemary, lavenders of various kinds, edgings of thymes and sweet marjoram, deliciously fragrant clove pinks, tall hollyhocks and in cooler areas foxgloves and the hardier upright fuchsias never fail to form a peaceful background to any garden and their charm is universal. The old roses with their inherent strength can tolerate competition from relatively dense plant growth, once well-established with good lengths of canes rising above the cover. In such a garden there are flowers throughout the year and bees and butterflies like living jewels move from nectar pot to nectar pot.

The hobby of collecting plant antiques is an infinitely absorbing one, and perhaps the one that offers most excitement of all is that of collecting old roses. It is not a new hobby, far from it. In the nineteenth century there were many avid collectors just as there have been in this century. Many hundreds of old roses have been restored to cultivation thanks to their efforts, yet so many more await rediscovery. The last representative of a once widely grown old variety may be your next discovery, perhaps a rose thought to be extinct. And as a result your name will be added to the history of the rose, and the world will once again grow, admire and smell a rose that might have been lost forever.

It isn't only the nineteenth century and older roses that are at risk of extinction. Many good older Hybrid Teas and Polyanthas from the earlier twentieth century are missing and may be lost. Yet many were glorious roses, only ousted by fashion and the desire to keep up with the newest varieties.

One we restored to our rose lists a few years ago, 'Laurent Carl', now has a tremendous following with its lovely deep red cupped flowers of incredibly rich damask fragrance, excellent vigour, health and floriferousness. Where today are great roses of the immediate past like 'Liberty', 'Hadley', 'George Dickson', 'American Beauty', 'Jules Margottin', 'General Macarthur', 'Hugh Dickson', 'Neige Parfum', 'Ellen Willmott', 'George Schwartz', 'Perle des Jardins', 'Grey Pearl', 'Portadown Fragrance' . . . the list is endless of roses on the edge of extinction or lost forever.

Many, but not all, of the old roses will take from cuttings which can then be grown on in spring in a nursery bed until they are of sufficient size (usually two years of age). They can then be lifted and moved to their permanent position. Moved earlier they often get lost among other plants and overgrown. That could be a tragedy bearing in mind how rare the plant may be.

Pencil thickness cuttings taken in early to mid-autumn will have the optimum chance of taking. Use large pots and fill them firmly with soil. Cuttings should be about 25 cm to 30 cm long and should be pushed deep into the soil so that only the uppermost two axillary buds ('eyes') are above the soil level. (The less stem exposed to the air the less danger of the cutting dehydrating.) Firm the cuttings down well, place in a cool shady position, and water regularly. Rooting hormone can be used prior to planting if desired. The firm semi-ripe wood of autumn is by far the best. Stems which have recently flowered should be used; the upper piece of the stem comprising the remains of the flower and one or two leaves below it are cut off, and a second, slanting, cut made 25–30 cm below. The second cut should preferably be made just below the insertion point of a leaf.

Earlier in the season, or in hotter areas, it is wise to construct a miniature hot house over the cuttings by using a large plastic bag; this should be held away from the cuttings to prevent rotting by the insertion of two pieces of cane or short lengths of stick and then secured around the edge of the pot with rubber bands. The pot should be put in a cool

shady place, otherwise in summer heat cuttings can literally steam to death.

It is wise indeed to pass on some material of anything likely to be rare to a specialist rose grower who will bud it for you. Many cuttings will take only with difficulty or not at all in some rose classes, and it could be a tragedy for the rose world if the specimen from which you took your cuttings, together with the material you collected were to die. So many rare old rose bushes fall victim to new building developments, herbicide damage, or owners digging them out without realising their historical value, that this is entirely likely. Budded roses are in general, although not always, more vigorous. Their root system is much older than the budded material so they will establish more reliably for you than the fragile early roots of cuttings. Once your budded plant is established, you can then take further cuttings at your leisure.

Many old rambler roses, Teas, Gallicas, Damasks and Chinas in particular, do very well on their own roots once established, and this was how they were handed on in many cases by early colonists. I grow a fair number of old roses on their own roots myself but rarely, indeed, have I taken the risk of not simultaneously budding them.

Budwood can be collected in autumn, winter or toward mid-summer. In spring and early summer, buds are actively shooting, and the wood is sappy and soft so that budwood (and for that matter cutting material) is unavailable. Collect short lengths of wood from the current year's growth, each with several tight unopened axillary buds (located at the junction of leaves and stem).

When on collecting sprees make sure each bundle of cuttings is tied together securely, one bundle to one plant, and labelled with as much information as possible: precise location, date, information on colour and type and identification as far as possible. Never leave it to the end of the day to write down the information. You will never remember. No-one ever does! Place each bundle of cuttings in a separate plastic bag and seal. On expeditions I carry an insulated drink container with 'cold bricks' so that cuttings and budwood keep as fresh as possible until I can get them back.

Often in late spring you will see an old summer-flowering rose in full beauty. Unless you make a careful note of exactly where you saw it so that you can return at the right time of year to collect it, you will lose it again for another year.

One last word on collecting old roses. They are

frequently associated with deserted areas over-run with long grass and, not infrequently in Australia, with snakes. A good pair of heavy boots may be inelegant but they save a great many frights when rustling is heard in the undergrowth! Look around old farmhouses, old cottages in mining towns and earlier settled areas, along roadsides and around fascinating old graveyards of the nineteenth century. Much has been lost but there is a treasure trove of old roses still to be found, many as beautiful as the roses described in the following pages.

Wild Roses

                                             . . .
                                    Oh, no man knows
              Through what wild centuries roves back the rose.

Appreciation of the perfection of simplicity is one of the evidences of true sophistication. It may well be that the increasing sophistication of rose lovers is evidenced by an upturn in popularity of the wild roses.

The gentle charms of the species roses and their hybrids requires an eye that has not been jaundiced by the searing colours and thickly-textured giant blooms of so many modern Hybrid Tea roses.

With relatively few exceptions the wild roses are in bloom for only a few weeks of each year, but that blooming is of such abundance, delicacy and charm that a year of flowers is compressed into a month.

Most of the wild roses are single and five petalled. They have all the delicacy and charm of a host of butterflies alighting in their thousands along every arching branch of the shrub. This cloud of butterfly flowers is in delightful colours, pale primrose, buttercup, palest pinks, rose, wild apricot, and the minglings of a dawn sky. Their singleness often reveals beautiful crowns of golden stamens, sometimes of amber, apricot or ruby.

The fragrance of the wild rose is untrammelled by man. They carry their wildness in their scent: the fresh sweetness of the eglantine and its progeny, diffusing on the air and made more sweet by rain, or the freshness of green apples, the piercing sweetness of the musk, the wild cowslip fragrance of the Yellow Banksia, the overwhelming wine and violets of White Banksia. To these must be added pure sweet fruit fragrances of orange blossom, lemons, ripe apricots or bananas. Others owe relationship to no other plants with their fine astringent dashes of sweet cool fragrance.

For those used to the inadequate foliage and gawkiness of Hybrid Tea roses, it requires a major reorientation of thinking to consider roses in terms of being foliage plants. Yet the great diversity and ornamental quality of the leaves of most wild roses is one of their finest features. Many have luscious ruby or grape-purple spring foliage, and a number are noted for their superb autumn coloration. Most modern roses when not in flower are a fairly distressing sight aesthetically, but you need never fear that the wild roses and their near hybrids will fail to contribute to the overall beauty of your garden when they are not in flower. Even in the summer months the foliage, from bold to ferny, is in a subtle colour range of yellow-greens, olives, rich greens, blue-greens and even silver-greens, the surfaces silky or rugose or shining. A mixed hedgerow of these roses presents to the discerning eye a subtle rich tapestry of colours and textures ringing the changes through three seasons, an admirable backdrop to the perennial flowers of high summer or to be appreciated on their own.

The riches of the wild roses for many reach their height in the autumn when the heps glow like cascades of jewels on every branch. No-one who has not seen a collection of wild roses in the crisp months of autumn can have any idea of the variety and beauty in rose heps. Plump polished wax red fruit like small applies vie with scarlet flask-shaped heps, polished ebony black clusters with jade green jewels, chestnut-burred heps with fountains of tiny rubies to produce an Aladdin's Cave of delights. If you can bear to part with their autumn beauty, the 'more practically minded amongst us may concoct all manner of delicious syrups, conserves, sauces and tarts to celebrate the end of the rose harvest.

'The first quality of the rose', said St Francis de Sales, 'is that it grows without artificial aid, and has hardly any need of being cultivated, as you see roses growing in the fields growing up without any cultivation.' We all seem to carry within us some hidden secret memory of the Garden of Eden. Repetitively through the history of gardening, despite the severity of design of some periods and the grand classicism of others, has resurged the desire for a Paradise Garden, a garden of only half-tamed beauty, rioting in a jungle of colour, fruit, fragrance and leafy retreats, a place for all creatures to live in harmony with each other. The wild garden as it was proposed by William Robinson and implemented by Gertrude Jekyll, and the modern schools of edible landscaping, organic gardening and native plantings are world-wide expressions in more recent times of paradise gardening. They have many counterparts in the history of past centuries.

The wild roses, the roses of the hedgerows, the fields, the mountain slopes, belong to our dreams of paradise gardens. They bring with them all the blessings of beauty, delicate colour, fragrance, glowing fruit, rioting generous growth and abundant cool foliage. They ask so little and give so much. They dislike all those things which are mandatory for most modern roses. They are better left alone, for they dislike pruning. As for spraying, such is their vigour that they shrug off pests and diseases. Never, never do I touch them. All they require from humans is appreciation.

Many think of wild roses as being suited only to the larger garden in the city, and to the country garden, by virtue of the size of the bush. The truth is, however, that wild roses come in all shapes and sizes and many are well suited to the smaller garden. As to the fact that the majority are once flowering, well it is true but so too are most of our cherished shrubs such as camellias, lilacs, viburnums and others. And the truth is that wild roses with their flowers, foliage and fruit pull their weight in a garden for three seasons of the year.

Rosa eglanteria (plate 18) is the eglantine or sweet briar of Spenser, of Shakespeare and all the old writers. 'The eglantine will cast a sweet and pleasant smell, although it reach not far off', wrote Pliny. Indeed it has perhaps the most pure and delicate perfume of all roses with a refreshing dash of coolness. The foliage and heps when touched by the fingers or after rain give off the scent of fresh sweet apples which reaches far and wide. The flowers borne along the length of the arching branches are single and pink, followed by glowing red flask-shaped heps which are retained for a long time. This rose laboured long under the name of *Rosa rubiginosa* meaning 'rust-coloured', which arise from a fortunately rare error in the work of the great taxonomist Linnaeus who accidentally transposed the names of the Austrian Yellow Rose and the eglantine. Fortunately its rightful title has

now been restored to this charming and ancient inhabitant of English gardens.

The eglantine was one of the sixteen kinds of cultivated roses mentioned in Gerard's herbal of 1597. Selected forms of the eglantine which differed from the normal wild form were introduced into gardens. English plant lists of the eighteenth century listed several varieties including double forms and William Paul, a reliable stabiliser in the rose listings of the earlier part of the nineteenth century, listed a total of fifteen garden varieties including a pink one with mossy buds called 'Mossy'. One of these 'varieties from the wild' is still offered in England. 'Janet's Pride' was found growing in a hedgerow beside a lane in Cheshire and was introduced by the nursery Paul and Son in 1892. Its flowers are semi-double and pink, with white radiating from the centre.

The eglantine rose obviously had potential for interesting hybridisation work, and the challenge was taken up by Lord Penzance of Godalming in Surrey. In 1889 at the annual Rose Conference, Lord Penzance read a paper on the 'delights and capabilities of the wild rose'. He proved his point by releasing a total of sixteen hybrids of the eglantine rose in 1894 and 1895 through the firm of Keynes, Williams and Company of Salisbury. He was in his eightieth year which proves the fallacy of the belief that rose-breeding must begin, if not in the cradle, certainly the day afterward. Most likely still to be found are 'Lord Penzance' with pale pink blended to primrose blooms in a fleeting display like ephemeral butterflies poised on the bush, and 'Lady Penzance' of deeper colouration than her lord, a coppery-salmon, and with deliciously aromatic foliage which Jack Harkness, that great rosarian and observant writer, speaks of as 'sufficient to haunt the garden, like an agreeable ghost on a damp summer evening'.

From a self-set seed of one of the Penzance hybrids, 'Lucy Ashton', came a lovely shrub rose 'Magnifica' which is otherwise known as *R. eglanteria duplex*. 'Magnifica' was introduced into commerce in 1916, and was in turn hybridised with the Hybrid Tea 'Joanna Hill' to produce the magnificent 'Fritz Nobis', one of the finest shrub roses in the world. 'Fritz Nobis' (plate 82) is very vigorous and healthy with arching growth flowering along the length of every branch; the large double crinkle-petalled pink blooms retain the sweet wild fragrance of its grandfather.

The wild Scotch rose (*Rosa spinosissima*) is a low

thicketing rose often no more than knee high. The clean-cut white petals of this single rose are framed against clear green foliage, and the fragrance is as clean and sweet as the breezes that sweep over its native haunts. The large round heps that follow the flowers are so deep a brown as to appear 'like exaggerated black currants'. The Scotch rose is protected by multitudinous bristles and prickles, and its foliage is fernlike.

> A rose, as far as ever seen i' the North
> 　　Grew in a little garden all alone;
> A sweeter flower did nature ne'er put forth,
> 　　Nor fairer garden yet was never known.

The Scotch Rose was known as the Pimpernel or Burnet rose in the eighteenth century and earlier. From a 1578 translation of a Flemish herbal *A Niewe Herball or Histoire of Plants* written by Dodonaeus comes the following. 'Amongst the knides of wilde Roses, there is founde a sorte whose shutes, twigges and branches are covered all over with thicke small thornie prickles. The flowers be small single and white, & of a very good savour. The whole plant is bare and low, and the least of al both of the garden and wilde kind of Roses.' John Gerard, the sixteenth century English herbalist knew of it too, saying that it 'groweth in a pasture as you go from a village hard by London called Knightsbridge unto Fulham, a village thereby'.

Like the eglantine rose, the Scotch Rose shows natural variation in the wild and these variants were introduced from early times into gardens. Cream and blush coloured forms were known and semi-double forms too. Robert Brown, a partner in the nursery Dickson and Brown of Perth in Scotland, used such forms to breed the first truly double varieties. There were eight in all, and they were released in 1802 and 1803. They were listed as white, yellow, two 'lady's blush', light red, red, dark marbled and bicoloured. Then a Glasgow nurseryman, Robert Austin, took on the challenge and bred from the Perth roses, eventually publishing a catalogue of 208 Scotch roses.

The vogue for these dainty elfin roses was not very long-lived but from it came one of the loveliest roses of all time, a rose for the heart. 'Stanwell Pereptual' was introduced in 1838, 'one of the prettiest and sweetest of autumnal roses' said Thomas Rivers in 1840. It is thought to have arisen from a cross between the Autumn Damask and the Scotch rose. The flowers are fully double, quite large, cupped with muddled centres and of a pure delicate pale pink colour. The fragrance is sweet and fresh. Unlike the other Scotch roses, 'Stanwell Pereptual' blooms on and on against delightful grey-green ferny foliage. It is taller than the Scotch roses and lacks the suckering habit. Jack Harkness considers it to be 'a beautiful rose . . . the essence of the old old-fashioned roses'.

The old Scotch roses make a delightful collection of their own and their names conjure up the past: 'Double Blush', 'Double Cream', 'Irish Rich Marbled', the fragrant single white Altai rose (*R. spinosissima altaica*), the rich pink fragrant Andrew's rose (*R. spinosissima andrewsii*), the very fragrant double yellow known as 'William's Double Yellow' of 1828, 'Mary Queen of Scots' with fat lilac-grey buds opening to rounded double plum-purple flowers with a paler reverse, 'Single Cherry' (plate 85), and 'William III', with rich crimson cerise semi-double flowers deepening to plum.

Three lovely pale pink forms are the double perpetual flowering 'Karl Foerster', 'Staffa' with semi-double blooms showing clusters of golden stamens and 'Falkland', a lilac-pink fading to palest pink in the sun and followed by wine-coloured fruit. But where, one wonders, is the 'Double Lady's Blush', or the French 'Painted Lady'?

Completely different from the typical Scotch roses above are a series of larger shrub roses bred by Wilhelm Kordes in Germany from crosses with Hybrid Teas. The result was some of the most beautiful and useful shrub roses we have: 'Frühlingsgold' (Spring Gold) (plate 45) sweetly fragrant creamy-yellow semi-double flowers, 'Frühlingsmorgen' (Spring Morning) with deliciously fragrant single pink blooms like those of the eglantine, shaded to cream in the centre, 'Frülingsanfang' (Spring's Opening) with very fragrant large single ivory flowers and wine-red fruit, 'Frülingsduft' (Spring's Fragrance) with large semi-double and very fragrant apricot flowers and 'Frülingszauber' ('Spring's Enchantment') with very fragrant bright cerise blooms followed by wine-red large fruit.

That great rosarian Roy Shepherd from Ohio, author of *History of the Rose* also crossed Hybrid Tea blood with Scotch rose blood to produce the superb 'Golden Wings' a large single very fragrant golden-yellow flowers with deeper gold stamens in the heart.

One other hybrid of the Scotch rose must be mentioned, 'Harison's Yellow' or 'Harisonii', introduced originally in New York c.1830 and said to have been found in the garden of a New York lawyer, George Harrison. It's most probable origin was the double yellow Scotch rose which has *R. foetida* blood in its composition.

The dog rose, *R. canina*, so frequently found in hedgerows in England and adding so much charm to the roadsides of South Australia, is a tall hardy wild rose of real prettiness with blushed single fragrant blooms followed by bright waxy red heps in the autumn. The term 'dog' incidentally was used to describe a plant of common occurrence in the old days so that 'dog violets' and 'dog roses' were simply the common species. The heps, like those of the eglantine and Rugosa roses, are rich in Vitamin C and are used to make rose hip syrup, often used as a childhood vitamin supplement. For adults, the news that the heps make a fragrant and delicious wine is equally welcome.

The dog rose was once commonly used as an understock on which to bud roses. Its marked tendency to sucker has put it out of favour however in this age of 'do it yourself' gardening. The story was different in more spacious eras when a gardening staff might well be employed by the private householders. *Rosa canina* was always greatly favoured for the production of that epitomy of Victorian garden plantings, the standard rose. Standard roses (known as tree roses in America, *rosiers tiges* in France, and even stem roses in parts of Australia) are budded onto long single-stemmed understocks in order that the roses may be lifted up for close sniffing and viewing and to add height to the garden. Those who know the writings of that great rosarian of Victorian days, Dean Hole, will be familiar with his cheerful resignation in facing the facts of life with his poor country parishioners. When the briar man was seen at church, Dean Hole was reminded of the need to place an order for his standard understocks. Once the order was placed, that particular parishioner was not to be seen in church for yet another twelve months, for the growing of rose understocks was a valuable supplement to the countryman's earnings.

Rosa canina, and the tribe of Caninae in general, have an unusual method of meiosis which is responsible for the very few hybrid or even varietal offspring available. 'Abbotswood' is a chance seedling which was discovered in a hedge surrounding a garden in Gloucestershire called Abbotswood. It is a rose of great beauty, an arching shrub to 2 m × 2 m with clear pink semi-double very fragrant blooms in abundance followed by handsome orange-red fruits. Semi-double dog roses have also

been known in the past. 'Andersonii' was one of Miss Willmott's favoured roses, a larger flowered form of the dog rose with richer colouring than the species. Miss Willmott spoke of it in her famous *The Genus Rosa* (1910–1914) as being found at that time in many old gardens. It was reintroduced by the great English nursery firm Hillier and Sons of Winchester in c.1935.

The number of ministers of religion who became enamoured of the rose seems excessive when compared with other professions in the nineteenth century. The Reverend Wolley-Dod is one such who gave his name to the semi-double form of the apple rose. *Rosa pomifera*, for many years called *R. villosa*, is a wild rose of unmistakable charm. The shrub is handsome and large with plentiful soft downy leaves that seem to shrug off disease, and flowers deliciously well described by Jack Harkness as 'clear and lovely, the rose pink of them full of kindness and good cheer, the petals slightly creased like new clothes not quite shaken out'. The flowers are followed by large, hairy red heps rather more like fat gooseberries in truth than apples. The semi-double form, thought to have originated before 1797, is equally charming and apart from acquiring the name of Wolly-Dod's rose is also known as Pomifera 'Duplex'. Both forms make superb dense hedges to 2 m or a little more.

Some roses are unmistakedly at risk from the flower arranger in the family. *Rose rubrifolia* should really be guarded day and night for its foliage has the rich purple red bloom of the grape upon it and it is for this, its gracefulness as a shrub, and the great bunches of wine-red heps in the autumn that it is chiefly grown. The flowers are fleeting wildlings, single pink with paler centres and golden stamens, borne in clusters. A hybrid, 'Carmenetta', introduced in 1930, and said to be a cross with *R. rugosa*, has slightly larger flowers and bunches of fruit, but this is offset by the acquisition of some thorns on the originally smooth wood and by its being less graceful.

The Cinnamon Rose (*R. cinnamomea*) is one of those old-fashioned roses that is still loved by those who know of it. Louise Beebe Wilder in her classic book *The Fragrant Garden* described it as 'a small, flat, tumble-headed pink rose of fine if faint spicy scent, often found flourishing by the dusty highway, or deserted gardens. Not now found in Rose lists but it was popular with our grandmothers who cherished many sweet and simple things'. It is one of the oldest of double roses (dating to at least 1569) and is one of Gerard's roses and a favourite of Tudor gardeners. It blends charmingly with wilder sorts of roses as well as the more 'civilised'. Like many old roses it has acquired many names including 'Rose de Mai', 'Rose de Paques', 'Rose du Saint-Sacrament', and *R. majalis*. Henry Phillips in his *Sylva Florifera* wrote, 'It is a favourite with our fair sex as it may be worn in the bosom longer than any other rose without fading whilst its diminutive size ... adapts it well to fill the place of a jeweller's broach'.

Like Jack Harkness, I am frequently amazed at the lack of interest expressed by writers in *Rosa californica plena* and must conclude that, as it is very variable in the wild, both poor and excellent strains are circulating. Indeed I have yet to find two descriptions which appear to coincide on anything other than that they are of double roses. Jack Harkness has apparently come to the same conclusions.

Probably the first American rose to reach European shores was *R. virginiana*. It was known to be commercially available in 1760 in England but 'Virginia Red' was referred to by John Parkinson in 1640. It is one of the most beautiful of the wild roses, gracefully mounding, with large cheery rich pink single blooms followed by glowing red heps. 'Rose d'Amour' (*R. virginiana plena* syn. *R. × rapa*) (plate 32) is suspected of being a hybrid of the Virginiana Rose rather than a variety. The exquisitely scrolled buds open to sweetly fragrant clear deep pink semi-double blooms. It was also known as 'St Mark's Rose'.

The old name for the Virginian rose was *R. lucida*, meaning shining, which was accurately descriptive of the almost translucent petals and glistening foliage.

The gooseberry-leaf rose also comes from America and is one of the quaintest of all roses. It builds up to a little thicket of pale green stems covered with tiny golden prickles and gooseberry-like leaves. The single rich pink blooms with a creamy boss of stamens and strange oriental fragrance are followed by plump amber-coloured gooseberry-like heps. The Sacramento rose (*R. stellata mirifica*) differs in having fewer stamens and red heps.

A trio of charming single yellow roses from Asia all deserve their place in the wild garden. The incense rose, *Rosa primula*, forms a quite low-growing bush with pale primrose single roses the length of its arching stems in spring, and deliciously aromatic fernlike leaves that smell of incense when touched; in heavy humid conditions the perfume can be detected without brushing the leaves. *Rosa ecae* was discovered by a British Army medical officer and botanist Dr J.E.T. Aitchison, while serving in the second Afghan War. The upright ferny-leafed branches smother in clear yellow single blooms in spring. A superb hybrid of *R. ecae* was bred from a cross with 'Canary Bird' and the result was a spectacular, graceful arching shrub with larger, fragrant, lovely golden single blooms and typical ferny foliage. It is known as 'Golden Chersonese' (1969). It was raised by E.F. Allen of Copdock and was one of Hillier and Sons introductions. It is now considered one of the most beautiful plants ever bred for the garden.

The third species in this delightful trio is Father Hugo's rose, once known as the 'Golden Rose of China'. It was discovered in China by the Rev. Hugh Scallan who was also known as 'Father Hugh'. The primrose single blooms along the arching stems have a wild and simple beauty of their own. A lovely hybrid which retains the charms of the parent is *R. x cantabrigiensis* which was raised in 1931 at the Botanic Garden of Cambridge. The flowers are pure, pale, perfect and frail.

From the ancient countries of the Middle East comes another group of glorious golden roses, but this time much in the style of the modern roses. The 'Austrian Briar' or 'Austrian Yellow' (plate 86), source of the yellow in modern roses, owes its connection with Austria only due to the report that Clusius brought it to Holland from Vienna in the 1560s. We now know that it was widely cultivated in the Middle East. It was known to John Gerard in his *Herball* of 1597, although his reflections upon its origin must be considered quaint, for he says it is 'by Art so coloured, and altered from his first estate, by grafting a silde Rose upon a Broome-stalke'. Nurseries lack that necessary touch of magic these days one fears. It would appear that John Gerard was right in suspecting human intervention in the development of this rose as it is virtually sterile, rarely setting seed. It has large, brilliant, unfading single blooms that still stir admiration in the modern garden. A marvellous double brilliant yellow, the 'Persian Yellow' rose was introduced to Europe from Iran in 1837 and immediately became the rage. It shares with the single form a strange incenselike powerful fragrance which does not at all earn the specific epithet *foetida*. 'Persian Yellow' has led to some spectacularly lovely roses including the climber 'Lawrence Johnston'.

The 'Austrian Copper Rose' or, as it is known in France, 'Rose Capucine' or 'Nasturtium Rose' is one of the most glorious blazes of colour in the rose world. It can, in many years, grow quite enormous as this reminiscence from the *Rosarian's Year Book* of 1890 reveals: 'One of the grandest, though but ephemeral, sights I have lately seen was the Copper Austrian Briar, in the garden of a village shoemaker, as big as a small haystack, and a blaze like one of Turner's sunsets'. All of which should prepare one for a rose with petals which are nasturtium red on the inside and golden yellow on the outside. It is clearly a sport of 'Austrian Yellow' and it occasionally reverts back to it.

The ancient sulphur rose or Hemisphaerica must surely at its best be one of the loveliest roses ever dreamt of. If there is any doubt then linger upon the glorious and faithful portrait painted by Redoute. All the large yellow roses of the world originated from the ancient kingdom of Persia which included what we now call Iran, Iraq, Afghanistan, and Turkistan. The Persian Empire stretched at one time from present day Spain to China. The opportunity for hybridisation and the development of wonderful roses from such diverse resources must have been very great and from such development must have arisen the sulphur rose. The full nodding yellow cabbage rose blooms and sea green leaves have much of *Rosa centifolia* about them, but we have no evidence of its origin, only a testament to the skill and good taste of those ancient rosarians. It has been called 'Yellow Provence', and a dwarf sport which was grown in France was known as 'Pompom Jaune'. Most regrettably, $R \times hemisphaerica$ is sterile so that no more forms of this lovely rose could be developed. In Australia, with the warmth and dryness characteristic of this continent, the sulphur rose flowers as gloriously as it did in its homeland. It would appear that an arts and crafts exhibition was held around 1600 in Vienna. A contribution from Istanbul featured double yellow roses which astonished everyone. The botanist Clusius inquired after these mythical beauties and was delighted to find that they were not the result of artist's license. Introduced into Europe it became a great favourite and a very successful florists' rose in the drier warmer countries such as Italy and France.

A lovely and ancient little rose should rightly complete this brief look at the wildlings of the rose world. The 'Threepenny Bit Rose' is a dear little thing, the tiniest of all rose flowers, hence the name, and they are borne on quite a tall plant in profusion. The flowers are sweetly scented and salmon pink, followed by tiny orange heps. It does perfectly well in shade, an asset among roses.

Wild Roses Aloft

I know a bank whereon the wild thyme blows,
Where ox-lips and the nodding violet grows
Quite over-canopied with lush woodbine,
With sweet musk roses and with eglantine...
William Shakespeare, *A Midsummer Night's Dream*

The wild climbing roses have that same sweet simplicity of their shrub relatives and equally as large a helping of romance. So many have come to us through the daring and courage of the great plant hunters of previous centuries in China, Burma, Japan and other places of nineteenth century mystery and adventure. Others came from colonial America, from the Middle East, from southern Europe and the north of Africa.

Like the wild shrub roses, the climbing wild roses are enjoying a revival with discriminating gardeners. They rarely look good when planted directly beside a home (although there are exceptions) or in a very controlled and 'civilised' area of the garden, but they are superb for that woodland garden, for a little glade, for a little wild spot cherished within the larger garden. And for those with larger properties, they are the answer to country gardens where all but the nearest gardens to the house must survive as best they can on rainfall once established.

To bridge the more sophisticated and the wilder parts of the garden are a group of double-flowered wild roses, the Banksias and the Banksia hybrid 'Fortuneana' (plate 2). The Banksias have the same quality that 'Cecile Brunner' has, the ability to touch the heart and to be known by name even to those for whom, in general, a rose is just a rose. They are sentimental roses, somehow evoking a whole Victorian age of posies and primroses. The single white and the single primrose yellow have their place, with clusters of fragrant single blooms of charming innocence.

The double white form of the Banksia rose known as the 'Lady Bank's Rose' (*R. banksiae banksiae* syn. *banksiae albo-plena*) was introduced from Canton, China in 1807 by William Kerr. It is a rambling rose of unique beauty bearing small double white cupped blooms in posylike clusters like double cherry blossom along arching thornless branches, and exquisitely scented of violets.

George Forrest, the famous plant explorer, wrote, 'I saw it in absolute perfection in the Lashipa Valley. Can you imagine a rose mass a hundred or more feet in length and twenty through, a veritable cascade of the purest white backed by the most delicate green with a cushion of fragrance on every side.' Fellow plant explorer and master of prose, Reginald Farrer, described seeing it like '... heads of snow with an intoxicating scene of wine, and violets and pure warm sweetness'. Dean Hole, that reliable rosarian, said it had 'a sweet perfume as though it had just returned on a visit from the Violet'. A huge plant of this variety at Tombstone, Arizona was reputedly the largest rose bush in the world 'with a spread of 4620 square feet'.

The Double Yellow Banksia (*R. banksiae lutea*) was introduced into England from China in 1827, having been discovered on a wall in Nanking by a Dr Abel. This old rambler, so common around homesteads and cottages of colonial days, bears endless little Victorian posies of double primrose-like flowers which have a delicate sweet cowslip fragrance and are of the softest buttery cream colour. The single form is *R. banksiae lutescens*. Like so many of the great Chinese rose introductions to England, the Banksia roses are ill-suited to life in most of England. They need the reliable, warmer, longer summers of places like Australia to ripen the flowering wood for the following flowering. Banksia roses should never be pruned during their years of establishment if possible, and, as flowers are borne on old wood, it is inadvisable to prune old wood out of the plant unless absolutely necessary.

The two single forms of Banksia roses, the buff yellow *R. banksiae lutescens* and the single white *R. banksiae normalis* are worthy of consideration also as linking features in the garden, ideal for scrambling over pergolas or archways. The single white is deliciously fragrant. Its Chinese name is *mu-lsiang* meaning 'white smoke' and it is native to central and southern China. It is assumed to be the wild species from which the single yellow form was selected.

Both double forms of the Banksia rose appear to be almost fully sterile. The single forms do set heps occasionally however and it is surprising that so little effort has been made to breed with this rose. The only success story is R. × *fortuniana*, a charming and fragrant double white with larger flowers than the Banksia, rather like a white flowered Cecile Brunner in size and form, smothering a dark shiny-leafed climber. It is the epitomy of old-fashioned roses and is always accorded much admiration in its season, which is relatively early as with its Banksia parent. It arose from a cross between *Rosa laevigata* (plate 1), the Cherokee rose, and *R. banksiae*.

The Cherokee rose was an old favourite in colonial gardens. It is a common wild rose in China and has become naturalised in the southern United States where it is often mistakenly believed to be a native, hence its name. The state of Georgia has taken it sufficiently to its heart to make it the state floral emblem. In France the large single milky white blooms with their golden boss of stamens and clove-like fragrance earned the name of the camellia rose. It has at least seven additional synonymous Latin names of which the most commonly encountered is *Rosa sinica alba*. The Cherokee rose is a vigorous, shiny, dark-leafed climber and will cover quite an area if necessary. It was introduced into England in 1759.

A pink-flowered hybrid of the Cherokee rose was released in 1896, bred by J.C. Schmidt of Erfurt in Germany. The pollen parent was reputedly a Tea rose. It has large soft pink silky single roses of perfect formation and strong sweet scent. It is, apparently, fully sterile but it did produce a deeper coloured sport called 'Ramona' (1913) which is also known as the 'Red Cherokee'. The Pink Cherokee rose has a number of different names which can be confusing. It is, among others, known as the Anemone rose, Sinica Anemone and in France *'Rosier Caméla à Fleurs d'Anémones roses'*. Both the Pink Cherokee and Red Cherokee are vigorous climbers in the style of *R. laevigata* (plate 1).

Another fabulous climber coming from the Cherokee rose stable and bred in this case by the distinguished American rose breeder Dr Walter van Fleet of Maryland is 'Silver Moon'. It is one of the most vigorous of all climbing roses, easily reaching 10 m if that is required, and excellent for climbing into a tree. The creamy buds open to large, slightly double white blooms with creamy shadows filled with the rich fragrance of ripe apples. The foliage is dark green, glossy, and magnificently healthy and in warmer climates such as ours the profusion of bloom can be breathtaking.

The Macartney rose, *R. bracteata*, is another splendid contribution of China to the world's great heritage of roses. It was collected by Lord Macartney during a diplomatic mission to China and entered England around 1793. Like the Cherokee rose, it took immediately to the warmer climate of the south of the U.S.A. where it has become naturalised. The fragrant flowers are big, single, saucer-shaped and moon-white with glowing golden stamens. In most warmer areas it is an evergreen with very glossy, dark green leaves. Like other roses mentioned in this chapter, the Macartney rose has fared ill at the hands of botanists and has been designated as *R. macartnea* and *R. lucida* which are now synonymous for *R. laevigata*.

Two outstanding hybrids have been developed from *R. laevigata*, 'Mermaid' and 'Marie Leonida'. 'Mermaid' is generally acknowledged by those who know their roses to be one of the great roses of all times. It was introduced by William Paul of Waltham Cross in England in 1918. The flowers are huge ('never ... had five petals covered so much space and conveyed so much beauty'), single, in a pure light primrose with a crown of amber stamens. It repeat flowers and is enormously vigorous, easily climbing into and cascading out of a tree. It is slow to establish but thereafter romps away, and is very resentful of pruning.

'Maria Leonida' was first mentioned in France in 1832 and was described as growing in England by 1840. The creamy white blooms are fragrant. It would appear that the present day rose is not the original one so named, although of the same period. It is generally known today as *R. × leonida* or sometimes Leonida.

Rosa filipes is a tremendously vigorous rose which needs to be trained up a tree or something equally tall, for it is perfectly capable of putting on 6–7 m of growth in a single growing season. The proviso however is that the rose should be sited away from the trunk, under some sturdy branches, and that proper feeding and plenty of water be used in the establishment years as the ground beneath trees is generally drier and more drained of nutrients. *R.*

filipes bears huge quantities of single creamy white blooms that are very free of their scent which resembles a rich spicy incense. The form 'Kiftsgate' is the one most commonly grown and will reach 7 m × 7 m in suitable conditions. *Filipes*, by the way, comes from *filipendula* meaning 'hanging from a thread', which refers to the roses' thin flower stalks.

Rosa longicuspus, like *R. filipes*, is an enormously vigorous rose from the Himalayas, to 7 m, bearing huge masses of creamy white flowers with the almost unbelievable and delicious scent of ripe bananas. *Rosa helenae*, named for the wife of the great plantsman E.H. Wilson, a fitting companion, bears as many flowers, but in denser heads and is likely to be the first into bloom. It has a strong spicy fragrance.

The Musk rose (*R. moschata*) reached England, reportedly, from Italy by the good offices of Thomas Cromwell prior to 1540 (which was when he lost his head, literally) and it was by all accounts one of the commonest of garden roses in Elizabethan and Jacobean times. The true Musk rose is very free of its fragrance giving off a true musk-like perfume. This was the rose of poets and playwrights, its fragrance and beauty extolled by such connoisseurs as Shakespeare and Francis Bacon. From all accounts this rose became virtually extinct in the nineteenth century for whatever reason no-one seems to know. It would appear that for a plant to possess a musk scent is a dangerous thing, for everyone knows that the musk flower lost its perfume too.

The true Musk rose was certainly grown in Ispahan where it was known as the Chinese Rose Tree. Seeds of the plant grown in Paris proved to be *R. moschata*. The Musk rose of the old herbals was an autumn flowering rose with oval leaves and it would seem that this was the true Musk rose.

John Gerard (1597) said of it, 'The Muske Rose flowereth in Autumn, or the fall of the leafe: the rest flower when the Damask and red Rose do'. John Parkinson (1629) described single and double forms of *R. moschata*: 'The Muske Rose, both single and double, rise up oftentimes to a very great height, that it overgroweth any arbour in a garden, or being set by an house side, to bee ten or twelve foote high, or more, but more especially of the single kinde, with many green farre spread branches, armed with a few sharpe great thornes, as the wilder sorts of roses are, whereof these are accounted to be kindes, having small dark green leaves on them, not much bigger than the leaves of Eglantine: ... the double bearing more double flowers, as if they were once or twice more double than the single with yellow thrummes also in the middle, both of them of a very sweete and pleasing smell, resembling Muske.'

What of the rose of Francis Bacon and Keats? The rose of the poets was summer flowering and is now thought to have been a deliciously fragrant white hedgerow rose, *R. arvensis* (plate 25), which flowers in England in July.

Those who are familiar with Mrs Gaskell's writings may recall in *My Lady Ludlow* 1859, 'That is the old Musk Rose, Shakespeare's Musk Rose, which is dying out through the Kingdom now'. By 1895, Cannon Ellacombe was saying in *In a Gloucestershire Garden* that 'The Musk Rose is not a very attractive rose, and is now very seldom seen, having been supplanted by its near relation *R. brunonii* (plate 21) from Nepal, probably only a geographical variety of the old musk rose'.

E.H. Wilson, a noted botanist, plant collector and gardener, whose opinion is therefore to be respected, wrote, 'The original Musk Rose, *R. moschata*, appears to have been a native of the Pyrenees, but has long been lost to cultivation, and its name applied to a vigorous climbing rose (*R. brunonii*)'.

For some reason, then, the original fragrant autumn Musk rose lost favour by the beginning of the nineteenth century, and was gradually supplanted by the much larger summer flowering *R. brunonii* which is easily recognised by its long drooping downy leaves. This latter is the Musk rose of Miss Willmott and of Bean.

Which all leads us to that most charming of English garden writers, the great E.A. Bowles who, in *My Garden in Summer* says, 'The true and rare old Musk Rose exists here, but in a juvenile state at present, for it is not many years since I brought it as cuttings from the splendid old specimen on the Grange at Bitton and I must not expect its deliciously scented, late in the season flowers before it has scrambled up its wall space'.

G.S. Thomas, who unravelled the mystery of the old Musk rose with all the detective skills needed to prove he would have been a decided asset to New Scotland Yard, went to E.A. Bowles' home, Myddelton House, in late August, 1963 and 'there on a cold north-west facing wall of the house was a rose just coming into flower. It was without doubt the Old Musk Rose. I had walked straight to it'. From this specimen G.S. Thomas took both cuttings and material for budding. The budded material flowered in their first season and, as G.S. Thomas explained, were to his amazement double flowered forms which exactly resembled the portrait by Redouté. Bowles' rose was a single so that, in one go, G.S. Thomas was rewarded with the spontaneously sported double form of the rose (apparently a common event in the past) as well as the single form. This material has since been disseminated by Graham Thomas. Our own shrub bears both single and double flowers in profusion.

One last thought on the Musk roses, both original and Himalayan. Musk perfume today seems to denote a heavy, rather sickly sweet penetrating odour. The Musk rose possesses a fragrance very close to that obtained from the musk deer, a fabulously expensive perfume which is refreshing and sweet, and not at all heavy and sickly. Even the word 'musk' seems to be changing its meaning. I repeat, anything labelled 'musk-scented' seems to be doomed!

The famous Musk Hybrids, which are mainly shrubs, deserve mention elsewhere, but one old hybrid should be mentioned here, *R.* × *dupontii*. In old books it was not uncommonly referred to as *R. moschata nivea*. Under any name it is well worth the struggle to obtain this rose. It grows into a spreading shrub which literally smothers with single milky-white large perfect flowers, shading to gold at the centre, with stunning ripe banana fragrance. It is a hybrid between *R. gallica* and *R. moschata* and was named after the head gardener for the Empress Josephine at Malmaison, André Dupont. More than one authority considers this to be the finest shrub rose of all. It has been in existence since at least 1817.

In the Royal National Rose Society's garden in England is a rose called 'Paul's Himalayan Musk'. It would appear to have *R. multiflora* in its bloodstream, and smothers in a veil of tiny pale lilac pink blooms.

'Francis E. Lester' (plate 87) (1947) must surely be one of the greatest climbing roses ever bred. It was developed by hybridisation with Mr Lester's favourite rose 'Kathleen'. There is unbelievable vigour derived from its Musk rose origin in this rose that climbs for the sky. The huge flower clusters of 25–30 blooms, each 5 cm or more across, open pale pink and white like apple blossom, then drop cleanly. Masses of brightly coloured heps follow. It fills the garden with an intense fragrance of bananas and oranges and for those in extremely cold areas, it is very, very cold resistant.

Rosa gigantea (plate 10) is another fabulous native climbing rose from China, and also from Burma. It was introduced into England in 1880 after its discovery by Sir Henry Collet in the Shan Hills in Northern Burma. It has very large pure white, fragrant single roses beautifully set off by very glossy deep green foliage. A form of this rose known as 'Cooper's Burmese Rose' or sometimes just 'Cooperi' was raised in 1931 at the National Rose Society's Trial Ground in England from seeds collected by Mr Cooper in the wild in Burma. This variation on the theme of *Rosa gigantea* has single pure white large blooms in the style of the Cherokee rose and extremely glossy dark green leaves.

The Roses of Summer

... there the dews
Are soft beneath a moon of gold
Here tulips bloom as they are told:
Unkempt about those hedges blows
An English unofficial rose.

Rupert Brooke (1887–1915), *The Old Vicarage, Grantchester*

Until the nineteenth century the last rose of summer was a genuine sadness. Roses bloomed for only two brief months, a little longer if the summer was kind enough to extend into an Indian summer when autumn drew on. As they commenced blooming in the first official month of summer, they were often known as the June roses. The roses of summer were the Gallicas, the Damasks, the Albas, the Centifolias and Mosses.

The Gallica roses were the first of the 'civilised' roses, the first to be cultivated by man. The Gallica rose was thought to have originated in Asia Minor and several forms were certainly known during the great days of the Roman Empire.

The red rose which is now known as *Rosa gallica officinalis* possesses the unusual property of preserving its fragrance long after it is dried. The rose petal has useful medicinal properties. It is both antiseptic and astringent. It was long part of many European pharmacopoeias and one town south-east of Paris, Provins, became famous as a centre of a trade based on the Gallica rose or Rose of Provins as it became known. For almost 600 years, people streamed into Provins for syrup of dried roses, honey of roses, electuary of roses, vinegar of roses, conserve of roses and other rose-based products. The Apothecary's Rose, as it became known, is still to be found in gardens today. It is also known as 'The Red Rose of Lancaster' as it became the symbol of the House of Lancaster in the unromantic, although romantically named, Wars of the Roses.

That lovely garden once created by the Empress Josephine at Malmaison housed most of the treasured Gallicas of the horticultural world and in fact most of the roses then known. There is nothing left of this garden for the lover of old roses but fragrant ghosts. Once it held such delightful Gallicas as the 'Pomegranate Rose', the 'Blue Provins Rose',

'Rose of Orleans', 'Sultana's Rose', 'Royal French Rose', 'Gigantic French Rose', 'Apothecary's Rose', 'Marbled Rose', 'Rose of Love', and the 'Purple Velvet Rose'. Some of these are still in existence in French and other collections, and a few such as 'Sultana's Rose' ('La Belle Sultane' or *R. gallica maheka*) and the Apothecary's Rose ('Red Rose of Lancaster) (plate 53) may still be obtained from specialist growers.

All the summer roses are naturally thicketing roses and will gradually form a large clump by the production of suckers if grown on their own roots, or in grafted plants if the bud union is buried below the ground. Where space is a problem, grafted plants with the union above the ground are advisable as no suckering of the budded plant will occur. (For the less expert, it is also helpful to be able to see the bud union and to know that any suckers emanating from below the bud union must be from the rootstock and may therefore be removed forthwith and with impunity.)

Few of the old June roses survive around Sydney from original plantings. One might assume from this that the climate was perhaps too warm or too humid for them to flourish unaided—until one looks at old cemetery plantings! Here, where fashion cannot touch them, huge suckering clumps may often be found, despite regular fires passing through, various mechanical monsters and total neglect. Only where herbicides have been employed do they fail to survive. No, around Sydney it is obvious that fashion, urban sprawl, keeping up with the times and the Jones's spelt the death knell of most of the colonial plantings. It is a delight to see the number of old homes in Sydney and its surrounding towns now being restored by those sensitive to and appreciative of the charms of the past. More often than not, once the house has been restored, the garden too is restored to its original form or recreated in an authentic period reproduction to house those simple, abundant, undemanding fragrant plants of the past that were such consolation to the settlers of colonial Australia. Where once such elegant old homes and gardens were unfashionable, they are not only now appreciated but valued and that value is expressed in enormously increased property valuation. Australia is at last beginning to appreciate her colonial heritage.

Identifying the group to which an old rose belongs can be fun. As E.E. Keays said, 'To examine these special points of distinction develops into as good a game as distinquishing Jacobean and Chippendale and Sheraton chair legs or Staffordshire borders on old blue plates!'

The clues to a Gallica's identity are many and older Gallicas will conform in the great majority of points. Outbreeding with other groups has obviously occurred however and it should not be surprising to find roses with predominant Gallica characteristics but not conforming exactly to type. As well, the Gallicas set seed with the greatest ease and seedling forms crop up which may puzzle the experts who hope to identify them.

The form of the Gallica is a quite low-growing (to about 1 m) thicketing bush formed of fairly stiff upright canes armed with weak, sparse straight prickles, some longer and some fine and small. The leaves are thick, dry, leathery, dull green, with five leaflets, finely dentate below and the petiole is finely beset with prickles. Gallica blooms are predominantly pink to rose pink to deep crimson, often with a lilac to plum purple cast. They are essentially gay, very floriferous and very tough and striping, marbling and flecking comes very naturally to them.

There were once so many lovely Gallicas to choose from. William Paul in his famous book *The Rose Garden* presented a selected list of 471 Gallicas and 52 Hybrid French Gallicas. The total number bred at that stage may well, according to various calculations, have been five times as many. Paul said of the Gallicas, 'All hues are here and the flowers are remarkable for their brilliancy, fullness, perfect outline and the regularity in the disposition of the petals ... and sweetness'.

Some of the loveliest pink roses the world has ever seen are among the Gallicas, huge fluffy very double creations, like glorious Edwardian chiffon roses that once decorated old-fashioned picture hats. They look unbelievably beautiful spilling out of full summer vases. Their fragrance is stunning.

Among them are 'Belle Isis' (plate 37) (1845) smothering with creamy pink fragrant blooms a little more blushed in the centre, the marvellously fragrant big cupped pale pink 'Duchesse de Montebello' (1829), the big quartered pink fragrant 'Blush Gallica' (also known as the 'Blush Damask') and the exquisite 'Duchesse d'Angoulême' (or 'Wax Rose') of 1836 with nodding very full saucer-like blooms of exquisite form and great sweetness.

Richer in colour is 'Empress Josephine' of very early origin with luxurious huge double blooms in rose with a lilac flush. It was first mentioned in the literature in 1853. 'Gloire de France' (1819) is a lighter pink with a distinct rose-lilac cast over the central petals, paling to creamy pale on the outer petals. In the lilac-pink range are two of the most exquisite roses ever bred, 'President de Séze' (Mme Hébert) (plate 23) bred before 1836 and 'Jenny Duval'.

My own 'President de Séze' in rich basalt soil has exceeded all growth expectations being around 1.8 m. In most gardens I think it would be more likely to reach between 1.2 and 1.5 m. It smothers in exquisite buds which unfurl slowly and perfectly to reveal a fully double bloom muddled and quartered in the centre with scrolled guard petals, in a luscious blend of rich rose pink overlaid with lilac and paling around the edges. The weight of the blooms bow down the stems into fragrant arches during the late spring and early summer. 'Jenny Duval' (the original name being lost) is an exquisite rose of rare colouring and undeniable beauty. The large very double fragrant flowers continually change colour during their development from dove grey and lilac to rich rose and parma violet to pale lavender pink.

In the rich velvety glowing dark crimsons are the 'Old Velvet Rose' (Tuscany) (plate 60) of c.1596 and 'Tuscany Superb', a little more double but lacking the marked contrast of rich gold stamens and velvety red petals, and the stunning 'Sissinghurst Castle' discovered by Vita Sackville-West with large very double plummy-rich red blooms and sweet fragrance. In the same lush colour range is 'La Belle Sultane' (1824) painted by Redoute, a large almost single rose with waxy petals in the richest, glowing velvety crimson, shaded almost to black, with a mass of golden stamens. Growing to 2 m this is one of the most sumptuous roses ever bred. It has also been named 'Violacea', 'Cumberland', and 'Maheka'.

Worthy of a place in any garden is 'D'Aguesseau' (1837), the most brilliant red among the gallicas. Dean Hole wrote of it: 'sitting in the garden one summer's evening with cigar and book, and looking up from the latter during one of those vacant moods ... my eyes rested upon a rose. It glowed in the splendour of the setting sun with such an intense and burning crimson, the tints of vivid scarlet gleaming mid the purplish petals, as light in jewels or in the dark red wine, that I shall never lose my first admiration for Rose d'Aguesseau (Gallica).'

'Duc de Guiche' ('Senat Roman') of 1835 is tall-growing for a gallica (to 1.5 m), a glorious opulent rich rose with very double globular flowers expanding to large almost reflexed blooms of unrivalled plushness in rich deep crimson, quartered with a tiny green eye. I would imagine the blooms might make the most tempting and fragrant bed ever designed for a fairy. It is the floral equivalent of sinking into a deliciously plump feather bed. The rose bows down with the weight of its early summer blooms.

'Hippolyte' is another sumptuous Gallica, a very old rose and probably a hybrid form growing nearly 2 m with virtually no thorns. It bears long sprays of exquisite little very double flat blooms, quartered, reflexing almost to a ball with a button eye. The overall colour is a soft violet lit with crimson from within. It is a most charming and fragrant rose.

'Duchesse de Buccleugh' (1846) is on the grand scale, tall growing to 2 m with large flowers, lovely at every stage, opening to very double quartered blooms of deep rich pink paling to an exquisite lavender pink around the edges. A rose that belongs on old-fashioned wallpapers and fabrics, evocative of a whole era.

David Austin of Wolverhampton in England has been working for a number of years on the development of a series of roses bred from the old-fashioned roses, which would retain their colours, form and fragrance and combine this with the repeat flowering habit of the modern roses. He has called these his 'English Roses' and they contain many splendid fragrant varieties that should be in the gardens of all old-fashioned rose growers. One of these lovely creatures, 'Constance Spry' (plate 8), has been on the top favourite lists ever since it was released in 1961. It was bred from the Gallica 'Belle Isis' and has huge cupped paeony-like blooms of an ethereal luminous clear, pale pink with the fragrance of myrrh. It can be treated as a climber or allowed to

form a large lax bush and is one of the glories of the rose world. There is nothing to compare with its loveliness in early summer. 'Chaucer' (plate 68), with large, deeply-cupped, full blooms in a delicate shade of pink, has strong myrrh fragrance also on a bush of typical Gallica growth; while 'The Knight' has the classic old rose conformation of the Gallica, its petals ringing a luscious change of crimson, purple and mauve.

All the English Roses are worthy of planting. Others with the old world look, fragrance and beauty are 'Wife of Bath', with luscious warm pink opulent blooms of deep fragrance on a little shrub; 'Charles Austin', a beautiful, flat, very double, very large, quartered bloom in shades of apricot and yellow and very fragrant; 'Glastonbury' with large saucers of rich deep crimson petals and heavy damask fragrance; 'Canterbury' with huge, flat, semi-double blooms of purest rose pink and golden stamens, an airy translucent confection with a powerful myrrh fragrance; 'Shropshire Lass', which resulted from a cross between 'Mme Butter-fly' and the Alba rose 'Mme Legras de St Germain', has large, saucerlike semi-double sweetly fragrant blooms in a delicate pink on a neat shrub with alba foliage; 'Chianti', another cele-brated Austin 'English Rose', is a beautiful shrub rose with double cupped blooms of rich wine red with a delicious true rose fragrance.

Only two single Gallicas have entered into commerce and one of them, a Hybrid Gallica called 'Complicata' (plate 54), is deserving of a place in any garden suburban sized or larger. Despite the name, it is an exquisite large single bloom of glowing clear rose pink with paler centre and a central crown of golden stamens. It forms a large shrub which is a magnificent sight in full flower, covered in a mantle of glowing rose which is followed by globular orange heps.

Other glorious Gallicas worthy of a place in any collection are 'Charles de Mills', with huge very double luscious blooms in deep subtle glowing crimson, and lovely little 'Belle de Crécy' (prior to 1848) with its clusters of very double and very fragrant parma violet blooms which have exquisite form. Of the gay striped Gallicas, more will be said in the chapter on striped roses.

Like the Gallicas, the Damask roses are ancient and their origins now lost in time. They appear to have arisen from hybridisation between the Gallica rose and *R. phoenicia* on the one hand, leading to the

THE ROSES OF SUMMER

group now known as Summer Damasks, and on the other hand with *R. moschata* leading to the Autumn Damask roses. Both groups are undoubtedly of ancient derivation. The Minoan roses depicted in fresco-paintings excavated on Crete near the ancient palace of Knossus strongly resemble the rose now known as the Holy Rose of Abyssinia, *R. sancta* Richard, known today as *R. × damascena*. The frescoes date to probably 2000 BC and this is the earliest known representation of a rose in historical times. The same Holy Rose was found twisted into garlands in Egyptian tombs dating back to between the second and fifth century AD.

It is at most the putting together of a jigsaw puzzle of which half the pieces are missing, but best guess would have it that the Holy Rose was introduced from Phoenicia (Syria) into Abyssinia by St Frumentius, the Phoenician Apostle of Ethiopia, in the fourth century A.D. In any case it was certainly planted within the precincts of Christian churches within his diocese. The Holy Rose would seem to be the early evolution of the Summer Damask rose.

The Autumn Damask rose is likewise ancient and was renowned in classical times for its fragrance and twice flowering qualities. We hear of it on the island of Samos in the tenth century B.C. being used in the worship of the goddess of love Aphrodite, a cult which later spread to Greece and Rome. Those fabulous rose gardens of King Midas in Macedonia, described by Herodotus as having roses of sixty petals and surpassing fragrance, were undoubtedly inhabited by the Autumn Damask rose. The roses of Paestum, too, were Autumn Damasks as were the roses of Pompeii. They can still be seen on the surviving frescoes of the villas. The fragrance of the damask rose was treasured in the ancient world and captured, for medicinal use and also in rose water. It was grown for this purpose, apparently on a huge scale, in Syria in the tenth century.

The Autumn Damask rose has gained many names in its travels. 'Quatre Saisons', the Four Seasons rose, was one. In Cuba the same rose is known as the Alexandria rose, a name which survives from the Spanish settlers on that island in the sixteenth century. As well it is called 'Damascena Bifera', the 'Rose of Paestum' and the Pompeii rose. By all names it is a lovely and vigorous rose with very double quite large blooms in clusters, in clear pink with a rich fragrance. It flowers prolifically in spring and repeat flowers

reliably in autumn with occasional blooms in between.

A romantic little rose grown from seeds of the Damask rose gathered on the tomb of Omar Khyyam at Naishapur. This rose is little both in size and height forming very double quilled and quartered fragrant light pink blooms with a pronounced button eye. One wonders what effect the great poet's aura had on the Damask for this seedling is the only one not known to conform with a tetraploid number of chromosomes. 'Omar Khyyam' is a pentaploid rose.

> When Omar died, the Rose did weep
> Its petals on his tomb;
> He would be laid where North winds keep
> The Rose in freshest bloom.
>
> Anna Hills, 1884

Equally full of romance is the lovely 'Gloire de Guilan'. It was introduced into rose lists in 1949 but is a very old rose from Iran. It is a graceful upward growing shrub to 1.5 m or more with us, with large full quartered blooms in clearest and most beautiful pink with delicious fragrance. It was one of the great attar of roses perfumery roses in Persia. The glorious abundance of bloom is framed by fresh green foliage.

Other roses used for the production of delectably fragrant and expensive attar of roses were 'Ispahan' and 'The Rose of Kazanlik'. 'Ispahan' (plate 34), also known as 'Pompon de Princes' and 'Rose d'Ispahan', is certainly older than its first date of mention, 1832. It is an exquisite rose as it unrolls from the bud to reveal a very double clear rose pink bloom. It is very free flowering, coming in clusters, and blooming over a long period of time for a summer rose. 'The Rose of Kazanlik' (1689) or 'Trigintipetala', as it is sometimes known, is a lax plant to two metres bearing profusely lovely double clear rose pink blooms with muddled centres and delicious intense fragrance. It was used as a source of attar of roses in the Valley of Roses in Bulgaria, east of Sofia.

Two exquisite white roses must rival each other as the greatest white rose ever bred, 'Mme Hardy' and the much less well known but exquisite 'Mme Zoetmans'. 'Mme Hardy' (plate 80) (1832) has few peers in the world of roses. It is certainly not a pure Damask and some suspect it of having more than a dash of Centifolia in its makeup. On our soil it has reached nearly 2 m, bearing divine showers of buds with just a faint hint of pink that open to pure white cupped blooms, then to exquisite flat large very double blooms of perfect conformation with a tiny green eye 'like an emerald in the snow'. It is a sumptuous and ravishing rose that not a few authorities consider the most superb white rose of all time. It was raised at the Jardin du Luxembourg in 1832 and named after the director's wife, Mme Eugene Hardy. It has been said of it that 'There is something so jewel-like, so exquisitely perfect in the arrangement of so many pure white petals, it might well serve as a model for Tiffany'.

'Mme Zoetmans' (1830) rivals 'Mme Hardy' for beauty as anyone who has seen this rarer rose will agree. It is a rose that might have been fashioned from a froth of white silk for a lady's chapeau, an exquisite large, full, cupped bloom that opens creamy-white with the faintest blush, soon becoming pure pale creamy white with delicious intense fragrance. The plant is bowed down with its perfumed burden of white in the season. Paul (1848), who knew the roses of his era as probably no-one else, said of it, 'A beautiful rose, well worthy of a place in the most limited collection. The blooms, like those of 'Mme Hardy', are set off by foliage of a fresh light green.'

As if these were not enough, one more white rose must be added, 'Botzaris' (1856). This is a rare Damask rose which owes much of its exquisite beauty to its *R. alba* ancestor. Clumps of rosy plump buds with ferny sepals open to long, flat, creamy-white, quartered blooms with a button eye and lovely Damask fragrance. It is a lovely, lovely rose made of dreams.

A rose from the past is 'York and Lancaster' (plate 83) (1551) a pied bloom of pink and white in which parts or all of some petals are rose pink on a background of pale pink. It has a sweet fragrance and sweet and gentle face at variance with its association with the Wars of the Roses.

'The Painted Damask' or 'Leda' (plate 35) is a rose first mentioned in the literature in 1827. It is a very fragrant and distinctive old rose with plump deep russet-red buds that open to extremely pretty very double roses of milky white suffused with blush, the outer petals here and there appearing to have had their tips dipped into a pot of carmine rouge. There is a 'Pink Leda' too.

'Hebe's Lip' (also 'Rubrotincta' or 'Reine Blanche') is a Damask of this century, 1912. It has an innocence rarely matched in the world of roses, with large fragrant creamy white blooms with the tips of the petals rose red, and a centre of pure golden stamens.

Some of the loveliest pink roses in the world are to be found among the old Damasks. 'La Ville de Bruxelles' (1849) has one of the largest blooms among the old-fashioned roses, with full, flat, quartered blooms of a rich soft clear pink with a button eye and lovely fragrance. 'Marie Louise' (1813) was raised at the Empress Josephine's gardens of Malmaison. By any standards it is a glorious rose, the shrub weighted down by its burden of large double luscious very fragrant blooms of deep pink with a button eye. 'Coralie' is altogether charming with its branches arched over by the weight of fragrant soft pink cupped blooms. 'Celsiana' (plate 16) (prior to 1750) is both exceedingly beautiful and very fragrant. This very old rose has clusters of wide and open double pale pink blooms of lovely old-fashioned muddled form, silky texture and a cluster of golden stamens. It was painted, as is only right, be Redoute at Malmaison.

Richest in colour is 'Rose de Resht' introduced by Miss Nancy Lindsay, an old Damask with large very fragrant blooms of a bright fuchsia-red. It is compact growing with a very long flowering season. Nor should 'Oeillet Flamand' be forgotten, with very large very double fragrant flat blooms of a rich clear rose pink.

The Rose of Albion (*Rosa alba*) and its lovely pale progeny bring with them all the romance of English history. The 'species' occurs naturally in many places in Europe, particularly in Britain, earning for that island in Roman times the name of Albion. Its status as a species is in doubt, and it is now thought to have originated from a natural cross between the Damask rose and the dog rose (*R. canina*).

All the Albas have blooms that are milky white, creamy or pale pink, set off by healthy soft, grey-green foliage. They are wonderfully vigorous and require little pruning. Just remove any dead or overcrowded wood in late winter, and shorten back unduly long canes that may prove to be a problem by two thirds. In common with all the best loved and cultivated roses of ancient times, the Albas all have exceedingly sweetly perfumed blooms, followed by large heps.

'Great Maiden's Blush' is one of our oldest roses dating back to the sixteenth century or earlier. It grows to about 1.5 m tall and 1.2 m across in a graceful shrub burdened with double blush white blooms with a deeper pink centre. It has a strong sweet perfume. In France it is called 'Cuisse de Nymphe' while a slightly more blushed form is known as 'Cuisse de Nymphe Emue'. This is the *R. incarnata* of Miller and Turner's Incarnation Rose. 'Maidens Blush' is a slightly smaller form.

The 'Jacobite Rose' or 'Great Double White' (plate 69) grows to around 1.8 m high and almost as wide. In late spring to early summer it smothers along its arching branches with large flat very double white blooms which are very fragrant. So fragrant is it that it is grown in Bulgaria for the production of attar of roses. The red heps that follow are an added attraction. There is little doubt that this rose was the Jacobite emblem. Long after the Jacobite cause was lost, its supporters could be seen wearing this rose in their buttonhole on 10 June. It can be seen today engraved on surviving Jacobite drinking glasses used to toast 'The King over the Water'.

The White Rose of York (*Rosa alba semi-plena*) is an ancient and superbly healthy big shrub for the back of the border or as a specimen planting. It covers its arching branches with large semi-double milky white blooms with partly concealed golden stamens. Sheperd described it as being like 'a great mock orange when in bloom'. It is very fragrant.

A less double form again, *Rosa alba suaveolens*, has great elegance and is rather like a huge Philadelphus flower. This highly scented form was grown in Bulgaria for the production of attar of roses.

'Belle Amour' is surely one of the most glorious sights in full bloom in the world of roses. Legend has it that it was discovered growing in a convent garden in Germany. It is probably the most free-flowering of all the Albas with lovely pale salmon-pink semi-double blooms with a warm exotic fragrance.

'Celestial' or 'Celeste' is another magnificent big bush to 1.8 m high and 1.2 m across bearing masses of purest pink large rounded blooms of delicious fragrance. In full bloom the shrub has an etherial quality which is matched by few roses.

'Mme Legras de St Germain' is another large shrub to 2 m, almost thornless, with pale green leaves and huge saucer-like fully double white blooms with creamy centres. 'Mme Plantier' is less large, very free flowering, with creamy-white sweetly scented double blooms with the perfect regularity of a formal camellia.

Another glory of the Alba roses is the much sought after 'Königin von Dänemarck' ('Queen of Denmark'). It reaches 1.5 m in height and 1 m in width with deeply blushed buds which open to large, flat, quartered blooms of delicate creamy pink with a delicious sweet fragrance.

For those with little space, there are three small compact Albas which are ideal for the small garden. 'Félicité Parmentier' (plate 11) is a rose of enormous charm bearing masses of creamy buds which open to very double palest pink blooms with a rich fragrance of honeysuckle. 'Pompon Blanc Parfait' bears masses of sweetly scented blush-white pompon-like flowers set off by grey-green foliage. 'Jeanne d'Arc', a lovely little rose, bears large full double blooms of soft creamy white filled with sweet fragrance which contrast with soft blue-green leaves.

One last blessing is brought to us by these glorious and in many cases ancient roses. Unlike the modern roses, and indeed most of the world's heritage of roses, the Albas will grow to perfection in areas that are fairly shady. They are marvellous for fragrant cascading hedges for larger properties and make excellent windbreaks for smaller roses. And above all, they are superbly vigorous and disease resistant.

The Rose of the Painters ('Rose des Peintres') has gathered many names in its long life. John Gerard in his English herbal of 1597 spoke of it as the Holland or Province rose. The spelling was Gerard's and it is called today the Rose of Provence. It was also known as the cabbage rose, referring to the way the petals fold over the centre of the flower and so delay revealing it, and the hundred-petalled rose or *Centfeuille* or in Latin *Centifolia*. In France it became the *Rose d'Avignon* or the Troubadour's rose.

The research carried out by Dr C.C. Hurst into the origins of the Centifolias concluded that they were a complex group of hybrids evolved in Holland in the sixteenth century and improved on and perfected into the eighteenth century. The hybridisation appears to have included *R. gallica*, *R. phoenicia*, *R. canina* and *R. moschata*.

Many of the Centifolias have tall open growth, rather lax and tending to arch downward under the burden of fragrant blooms carried each summer. However, as G.S. Thomas said, 'Drooping is the very spirit of the Provence Roses' and I for one love their nodding gracefulness and generous great fragrant blooms. The smaller forms of Centifolia such as 'Petite de Holland', 'De Meaux' and 'Spong' are much more upright growing, as are the much larger 'Fantin Latour' and 'Paul Ricault'. At one time more than a hundred different varieties were listed commercially.

One rose has become known as the type-form of the Centifolias to most minds. So much so that it is often referred to as Centifolia. It is in any case a glorious rose and was immortalised by many of the old painters and exquisitely painted by Redouté at Malmaison. The huge very double cupped blooms of fragile pale pink petals hold greater depth of colour in their centre and glorious old rose fragrance. It is a creature of airy delicacy and has absolutely nothing to do with cabbages except for its cupped form.

A sport of Centifolia which produced marvellously fringed and divided sepals like a ferny green ruff to the base of the flower is 'Chapeau de Napoléon', *R. centifolia cristata*. The sepals give the bud the appearance of a French tricorne. This rose of 1826 opens to flowers of great beauty, clear pink, globular, very double and sweetly fragrant. It was first discovered in a convent near Fribourg in Switzerland. It has earned many admirers during the century and a half that have passed since its birth. E.E. Keays said of it, 'The Crested Moss has grace and charm no other rose has. Decorative crests are so arranged on the bud that they form a three cornered decoration and fluff out at the top like a little bunch of plumes. The breaking bud is exquisite. The whole picture is an instance of rose magic.' Constance Spry delighted in it, commenting on 'how charmingly the crested calyx lies within the curved hollow of the backs of the petals. This aspect of the flower has fascinated many painters, while James E. Hanscom called it 'a lovely rose which recalls to me the dignity and peace in the gardens of a bygone generation'.

The Centifolia seems to have been a rose prone to producing extravagant and quite delicious mutations. M. Dupont, who was in charge of the gardens at Malmaison during the time of the Empress Josephine, propagated two roses of extraordinary foliage: the Lettuce-leaved rose (*R. centifolia bullata*), which was also known as 'Rose à Feuilles de Laitue', and the Celery-leaved rose (*R. centifolia bipinnata*), which apparently comes reasonably true from seed, a low-growing shrub with leaflets that are crisped and curled like those of celery or parsley. This curious rose has relatively little vigour and apparently did better on *R. canina* understock than on its own roots. I do not know of it finding its way to the Australian colonies, and have certainly never heard of it being found surviving here. A pity really because, despite the difficulties of propagation, it is a lovely rose, if Redouté's painting is to be believed, with masses of pretty buds and typical rosy pink Centifolia blooms. It was described as being very fragrant.

'The Lettuce-leaved Rose' ('Bullata') or 'Giant Cabbage-leaved Rose' is equally charming, with unusually large bright green leaves puckered in the manner of the outer leaves of a lettuce and luscious pink roses with great sweetness and spiciness of breath. A trait that can be disturbing is the unexpected bronzing of foliage during late summer, which is perfectly normal and rather handsome, definitely not something to cause you to rush away for a chemical spray. The Lettuce-leaved rose was first mentioned in the first major horticultural journal ever published in Europe *Le Bon Jardinier*, in the 1813 edition. It has long been a great favourite among rose growers for its beauty.

'Fantin Latour' (plate 4) is my personal favourite of all the Centifolias. It is a complex hybrid, difficult to place, but with pure Centifolia blooms. It is healthy, strong, forming a graceful shrub well clothed in handsome foliage on which the great abundance of blooms are poised with typical Centifolia charm. It is a magnificent Provence rose with circular cupped blooms, which flatten on opening while retaining the cupped centre, the whole in a delicate pale pink, warmly blushed in the centre and filled with delicious fragrance.

Of a deep rich pink, 'Reine des Centfeuilles' (1824) is a very free flowering Centifolia, bearing masses of very double beautifully quartered blooms with button eyes and very sweet fragrance. 'La Noblesse' is a smaller Centifolia suited to the suburban garden, with warm rose pink blooms. 'Juno' (1847) has the exquisite form of the Centifolia and opens to a flat quartered bloom with button eye in a delicate blush pink.

A number of old Centifolias were lilac-pink in colour. 'Duc de Fitzjames' is a vigorous shrub to two metres in height. The blooms borne in clusters are beautifully quartered with a green eye. An old Centifolia passed down by cutting through a Campbelltown family would appear to be the very old 'Mme Henriette' with lilac-pink very double rather coarse quartered and cupped blooms in which the guard petals are shaded crimson on the outside and maintain, by their upright nature, the cupped form.

'Paul Ricault' is a relatively late development in

Centifolias, having been released in 1845. It is one of the most free-flowering of all, reaching 1.6 m when well grown and smothers in large very double blooms filled with fragrance in a rich soft pink. Like 'Duc de Fitzjames' it is to be found at Rookwood. It is fairly common along the roadsides around Adelaide where it creates bright splashes of colour in November.

'The Bishop' has small blooms of rather similar colouring to a great old colonial Gallica 'Anaïs Ségales'. The latter, now commercially available in Australia, is one that I have never personally collected, yet it would appear from Nancy Steen's experiences that it is a common rose in old New Zealand plantings. 'The Bishop' has quite small flowers of rich colouring, the very double blooms opening rich deep crimson and quickly acquiring washes of lilac, violet and then slaty grey.

Perhaps the richest colouring of all belongs to 'Robert le Diable'. This Centifolia has more than a touch of Gallica about it and is certainly a complex hybrid with the Gallicas. This is evidenced by the subtle gradations of colour which this rose passes through. On a small vigorous bush are borne, quite late in the season, beautifully formed fragrant fully double roses that are a luscious mixture of wine-purple, claret, cerise, pale violet and lavender-grey. Much larger, indeed one of the tallest of all roses, reaching two metres comfortably, with arching branches weighed down by huge paeony-like fragrant blooms, is 'Tour de Malakoff'. This rose shares 'Robert le Diable' colouring, beginning lilac-pink, then deepening to an intense Parma violet and fading to grey-violet. It has all the colours of a rich ancient tapestry.

What endless possibilities lie within the Centifolias. It was the Centifolias which were to produce the first Baby or Pony roses beloved of the Victorians, of which more in the chapter so named. Mottling, striping and marbling, evidence of Gallica affiliations, are seen in the group. One Centifolia I would love to discover was the old Steeple rose which regularly produced a second bud where the stigmas would normally be on this huge, very fragrant pink globular bloom, and often two or even three buds in a tier arising above the original bloom rather like a Chinese temple constructed of roses. It was apparently propagated by layering in order to maintain the stock true to form. It arose from a mutation of the largest of the cabbage roses, *R. centifolia gigantea*. It was found in old colonial plantings in Maryland, USA by E.E. Keays. Alas it has not yet come my way. Most exquisite and in some ways most extraordinary of all the strange mutations of the Centifolias are that group known as the Moss roses.

The Mosses are characterised by an extraordinary change in the sepals in which the normal glandular projections of the sepals and peduncle become greatly enlarged to create a winged and mossy growth. The mossing is sticky with delicious fragrance and nothing lovelier exists in the rose world than the unfurling of the bud of a Moss rose at that exquisite moment when the petals lie protected and fragile within an emerald green mossy casement.

The original 'Old Pink Moss' or 'Common Moss' (*R. centifolia muscosa*) is a rose exquisite beyond description, with blooms of the clear pink perfection of the 'Rose des Peintres', filled with wonderful fragrance, and surrounded by the fresh green mossing of the sepals as exquisite as old lace. Constance Spry said of it, 'the rose that *par excellence* inspired the composers of valentines and the decorators of china long ago. This rose has slender, beautiful mossed buds which open to the prettiest pink flowers borne on slender stems and the scent is ravishing'. A beautiful white sport of 'Old Pink Moss' originated with Shailer in 1790 and became known variously as 'Shailer's White Moss' or 'White Bath' or 'Muscosa Alba'. The exquisite buds are blushed with pink but open pure white.

The Moss roses are most worthy of the collector's passion and a number of these most Victorian of all roses have been saved, precious antiques from the past to be jealously conserved and passed on for the delight of further generations. It is difficult to single out favourites for each is a gem. 'Mousseux du Japon' ('Japonica') is the mossiest of all the Mosses, with plump buds entirely covered with clear green, dense, fragrant moss opening to semi-double mauve-pink fragrant flowers quickly turning to a delightful old-fashioned shade of soft lilac grey. The mossing extends way down the stems.

Almost as mossy is 'Salet' (1854), a vigorous bushy shrub to one metre or a little more with profuse spring bloom and good autumn reblooming. 'Old Pink Moss' and 'Shailer's White Moss' also rebloom in autumn in most years. The heavily mossed buds open large and wide to reveal fragrant clear mid-pink double flowers with golden stamens. 'Gloire des Mousseux' ('Mme Alboni'), a Moss of 1852, comes in much the same exquisite clear pink, but the blooms are enormous, full-petalled with a button eye, long-lasting, and freely borne in masses. It is deliciously scented.

One of the Mosses that earns much praise in our gardens is 'Mme Louis Leveque' (1874). This lovely lady has very fragrant, very large, full, cupped blooms in a subtle pink. Another lady of equal distinction, 'Mme Delaroche-Lambert' (1851), has exceptionally beautiful well-mossed buds with long leafy sepals opening to reveal vividly coloured blooms blended rose and purple, very fragrant, with beautifully scrolled petals. It repeat flowers very well for us in autumn.

Other lovely Mosses well worthy of inclusion in any collection are 'A Longues Pedoncules' (1854) with small, exquisite, lilac-pink blooms, 'Baron de Wassenaer' (1854) with very full fragrant light crimson flowers, and 'Eugénie Guinoiseau' (1864), with a delicious fragrant bloom compounded of soft grape purple and richy plummy tints, later fading to soft lilac-purple with a claret heart.

One of the most famous and best loved of the Victorian roses is the 'Old Velvet Moss' or 'William Lobb' of 1855 vintage. The well mossed green buds open to fragrant, very double roses in the most splendid royal velvety purple crimson, which fades in the most appealing way to softest lavender-purple.

Almost of equal fame is 'Nuits de Young' (1851), a favourite old rose of the darkest maroon with velvety black tones and a circlet of golden gems. 'Henri Martin' is equally resplendent with fiery, handsome, fragrant dark crimson blooms with petals arranged with camellia-like precision.

I will mention only four more of this most collectable and worthwhile group: 'Mousseline' ('Alfred de Dalmas') of 1885, a beautiful and repeat-flowering Moss with large, cup-shaped, delicate blush pink blooms and sweet scent; 'General Kléber' (1856) with elegant well-mossed buds opening to large clear pink, delightfully fragrant blooms with button eyes; 'Lane's Moss' ('Laneii') of 1846 with well-mossed plump round buds opening to very double, large old-fashioned blooms of richest pink, very sweetly scented with a tiny green eye; and 'Golden Moss', by no means gold but in its own way charming.

It should only be added that nothing could look more delightfully old-fashioned or appropriate than an underplanting of that quintessentially old-fashioned, fragrant herb, lavender. A mixture of Mitcham lavender (*L.* × *allardii*) in the background, French (*L. dentata*), Italian (*L. stoechas*) and green lavender (*L. stoechas* var. *viridis*) in the middle distance, and English and Dutch or spike lavenders and their cultivars in the front is always successful, creating a restful picture of age old charm. There will scarcely be a week in most of Australia when such a mixture will not yield a bunch of fragrant lavender flowers of one kind or another. If greater diversity is required, then the soft ferny green of Lad's Love, with its lemon and camphor fragrance, and various forms of rosemaries might well be added.

Luscious Bourbons and Glorious Hybrid Perpetuals

I have a garden of my own
But so with roses overgrown
And lilies, that you would it guess
To be a little wilderness.

Andrew Marvell

The introduction of the China roses in the nineteenth century was to produce many beautiful classes of roses. A lovely 'dead end' in rose breeding was the Portlands. The first of this short-lived group was 'Duchess of Portland' or more correctly 'Paestana', of which one parent is thought to have been the red Gallica rose, the other a China. There are two better known surviving Portlands, one being 'Compte de Chambord' with clear pink globular roses borne in fragrant abundance on an arching shrub. It was introduced in 1860. The other survivor, 'Jacques Cartier', is reminiscent of a very double camellia of a very pretty pink. It was introduced in 1868 but, alas for the Portlands, they were to be outclassed by the much more impressive Hybrid Perpetuals.

A different mating of the Chinas was to be much more successful, even more so than the American liaison that developed into the Noisettes. From a romantic passing affair between a common China rose ('Old Blush') and the Red Four Seasons rose, growing in hedges on the Isle of Bourbon (now known as Reunion), came a chance offspring that was to found the great race of Bourbon roses. It was to be discovered on Bourbon by a botanical traveller for the French Government. Or so the story goes. The same claims have been made for the island of Mauritius and for the Calcutta Botanic Garden. Whatever the final truth, 'Rose Edouard' was to found a glorious line, still thought by many old rose lovers to be the greatest of them all.

The seeds of 'Rose Edouard', sent by the curator of the Botanical Gardens in the Ile de Bourbon, found their way into the hands of Jacques, head gardener to King Louis-Philippe. From these seeds was raised the first Bourbon born on French soil, 'Rosier de l'Ile Bourbon'. It was semi-double,

brilliantly rose in colour, superbly fragrant, and rebloomed even more satisfyingly in autumn than in spring. The foliage was almost evergreen. These characteristics were passed on to the Bourbons as a class. In addition, the Bourbons had, one and all, superlative blooms in great abundance.

'Boule de Neige' (1867) is the only white Bourbon still likely to be found from commercial sources. The flowers are exactly, as the name suggests, like snowballs. The very double blooms open to a perfect circular outline, like an ivory white camellia, then reflex until they form a near perfect fragrant white ball. Expect it to reach 1.5–2 m in height, the graceful cane-like growth cascading with white 'snowballs'. The foliage is a perfect, glossy dark green.

Perhaps the most loved of all the Bourbons, even perhaps of all the old-fashioned roses, is 'Souvenir de la Malmaison' (plate 2) (1843). It gives almost ceaselessly large creamy-pink, quartered flat blooms, with a delicious spicy sweet fragrance that may sometimes smell unexpectedly of ripe bananas with cinnamon. Nothing could more surely evoke the past than this glorious creature. I am greedy enough to have her in several places in the garden, both in the bush and the climbing forms. 'Souvenir de la Malmaison' had a sport which is singularly unlike its parent. The sport occurred more than a hundred years ago and is almost single, of that same creamy-pink inside with delicate blushes on the outside. It has an exquisite form and very sweet fragrance and is a worthy rose in all respects. This is 'Souvenir de St Anne'.

Rival to 'Souvenir de la Malmaison' in fame and beauty is 'La Reine Victoria' (plate 90) (1872). The shrub is composed of long slender canes to 2 m, bearing masses of exquisite cabbage rose blooms with old rose colouring and delicious fragrance. A sport, 'Mme Pierre Oger' (plate 47) (1878), differs only in colour. The shell-like petals are cream, blushed pink toward the edges. On hot sunny days the blushing increases to produce a clear rose bloom. A third rose considered to be of perfect form is the lovely 'Louise Odier'. It bears great swathes of roses, and blooms several times in the season, the autumn blooms being perhaps the loveliest. Each rose is full, cupped and perfectly circular in outline, in a warm lilac pink and filled with delicious fragrance.

The fragrance of ripe raspberries is one of the delights of the Bourbon group and four of the more readily available varieties have it in abundance. 'Mme Ernst Calvat' (1888) is a handsome pillar rose that can be pruned to a shrub with huge cabbage-rose blooms of clear lovely pink. She represents the high Victorian period as few roses can and has delicious strong raspberry fragrance. 'Mme Isaac Pereire' (1880) is a luscious rose with enormous very full rich rose-madder, saucer-shaped blooms quartered in the centre. Like 'Mme Ernst Calvat' she is fragrant of raspberries and is generally rated the most fragrant old-fashioned rose ever bred. 'Adam Messerich' with semi-double cupped blooms of rich pink and 'Kathleen Harrop' with clear pink pretty double blooms with deeper pink reverse are both deliciously fragrant, too, of raspberries.

I have the Victorian's love of a great-headed rose filled with opulence and fragrance. A very catholic taste, I fear, for I delight equally in fragile wildlings. It is unfashionable to love great generous-hearted flowers, whether they be those great plates of dahlias our forefathers loved or ostrich-plumed old varieties of asters or Hybrid Perpetual roses. But I see them as comfortable flowers, reliable, warm-hearted, generous. There should be flowers and colours to suit moods. Delicate pale pink single eglantine roses may suit one mood, yet by afternoon I crave to bury my nose in an enormous bowl of rich fragrance.

The Hybrid Perpetuals are being collected again, but alas it is too late to be sure of the names of some. I have quite a few nameless ones gathered in. They may well gain a name as I continue to research them against the old literature and compare them with overseas reference collections. In the meantime they continue to give great pleasure.

I sometimes wonder about 'Paul Neyron' (1869). Mine is an enormous rich pink bowl of a bloom, the colour so distinctive that it was once known as 'Neyron Pink', and of delicious fragrance. Trevor Griffith, I am pleased to see, agrees with me in his delightful book *My World of Old Roses*. Yet so many books declare it to be scentless. This is probably one of those regrettable examples of one author making a mistake and the heresy being repeated endlessly by following authors.

'Frau Karl Druschki' (1901) is, on the other hand, agreed by one and all to be scentless. But what a rose! Huge, generous pink-tinged buds open to a glory of white, and oh how she flowers. The good Frau is still the standard by which white roses are judged. Where is the white rose of the Hybrid Tea class that could match 'Frau Karl Druschki' in the Hybrid Perpetuals or 'Mme Hardy' in the Damasks?

'Georg Arends' (1910) is the strawberry icecream rose. The luscious double blooms unfurl from exquisitely folded blooms and the fragrance is superb. 'Mrs John Laing' (1887) has full, large, richly fragment, glorious blooms and flowers on and on. Equally worth collecting is the charming 'Reine des Violettes' (1860), glorious 'Baronne Prévost' with big, bright pink, fragrant, quartered blooms, and 'Mme Victor Verdier' (1863) with big double rich pink blooms so fragrant you want to bury your nose in them over and over. And then there is 'General Jacqueminot' (1853), dear General Jack of colonial days, a great rose with deep crimson fragrant blooms and... No, this will never do. Just believe me. Like so many comfortable things the Victorians loved, these luscious creatures are coming back into fashion. Do try some.

The Striped Rose

Rosa Mundi

Why do I love striped roses? I don't know except that I am addicted to the lovely old Dutch paintings that included them in all their silken glory in great casual vasefuls that Constance Spry might have designed.

There is something charming about the striped roses. They are gay with their little streaks and stripes, no two blooms the same. Some remind me of Edwardian curtains, all opulent satin with crimson stripes, some are very chic and French, others like a child might paint. So many seem to share my love of pied blooms. Gathered into this chapter are all the favourite striped old-fashioned roses.

First on any list of striped roses must be 'Rosa Mundi' named for Fair Rosamund, the mistress of Henry II who was King of England from 1154 to 1189. She was the daughter of Sir William de Clifford. Henry was obliged to marry elsewhere, a European princess long intended for him. The princess would brook no rivalry and arranged for Rosamund to be eliminated. The story goes that Henry was utterly overcome with grief. At his orders she was buried at Godstow Nunnery near Oxford where each year on the anniversary of her death the grave would be covered in her rose. 'Rosa Mundi' is an ancient rose, a sport of the Apothecary's rose, said to have been brought into England by the conquerors returning from the Holy Land. It is the gayest of roses, flowering but once a year, but smothering then in charmingly informal semi-double blooms of light pink, light red and white stripes with golden stamens. No two blooms are alike.

The Gallicas seem to have the ability to produce lovely striped roses. 'Camaieux' (1830) is one of the most beautiful of all the striped roses, a satiny creature with camellia-like blooms striped and splashed with creamy white, crimson, pink, lilac and grey. 'Tricolore de Flandre' (1846) makes a superb healthy plant bowing down with its weight of fragrant luscious cupped blooms striped with crimson purple, rose pink and lilac. 'Georges Vibert' (1853) looks like a rose-bush smothered in paper carnations. The fragrant blooms are light pink, white and light red with pinstripes of purple-red.

'York and Lancaster' (*R. damascena versicolor*) was first mentioned in 1551 and may be much older. It is a rose of fleeting loveliness, not striped as in the other roses but with some petals half rose pink, half white, others wholly white or pink. The fragrance is sweetest old rose. Its colours represent the colours of the roses used as the symbols of the House of York and the House of Lancaster.

The Centifolias can boast one outstanding striped rose that has been so much loved that it has acquired many names. 'La Rubanée' (plate 73) is perhaps the best known but it has been treasured for generations as 'Village Maid', 'Cottage Maid', 'Panachée à Fleurs Doubles', 'La Belle Villageoise' among others. It is such an endearing rose, like a milkmaid in a striped apron to my mind. The full and lovely blooms are filled with delicate creamy white petals so neatly striped with a fresh lilac pink. She flowers so freely and smells so sweet. Who could resist her?

The Moss roses, too, produced their striped lady, a dear small creature called humbly and simply 'Striped Moss', although in France it was a little grander as 'Oeillet Panachée'. It grows to only a metre in height, with small double fragrant white blooms striped pink and light crimson. When exactly it originated is not known, but it is certainly older than the year 1800.

Some of the loveliest of all striped roses are to be found among the Bourbon roses. How well stripes go with those fragrant luscious blooms. 'Variegata di Bologna' (1909) brings gasps of pleasure from almost all who ever see her—what a pleasurable burden of fragrance weights down her branches, what a glory of double cupped, pure white, silken blooms striped and splashed deliciously with crimson purple. Less dramatic but so truly old-fashioned is 'Honorine de Brabant' (plate 71). The lovely fragrant cupped blooms shower from the bush in pale pink, striped with lilac and crimson.

'Commandant Beaurepaire' (1874) makes an admirable third in this lovely trio. It is outstanding among striped roses, very fragrant with beautiful double cupped blooms of carmine-pink, handsomely striped with rose-madder, purple and occasionally slashed with brilliant red.

To all these lovely creatures must be added two wonderful Hybrid Perpetuals. 'Ferdinand Pichard' must surely have been a model for those lovely striped roses which once embellished beautiful shady hats in more elegant days. The lovely blooms are pale pink, striped with red and white and spilling fragrance. 'Vick's Caprice' (plate 63) (1897) is said to be a sport of the great old Hybrid Perpetual 'Archiduchesse Elisabeth d'Autriche'. It is quite a modest grower, easily accommodating to the smallest garden, with lovely globular cabbage blooms extravagantly striped pink lilac, white and rouge red.

Tea Scented Roses

Once upon a time, in far-off magical China, were bred the ancestors of all the Tea roses. Speculation would nominate *R. chinensis* and *R. gigantea* as the roses hybridised by those far off horticulturalists and the hybrid species has been designated *R.* × *odorata*. From their blood has sprung a race of roses, once designated as Tea-scented China roses, which has been acclaimed by so many as the crowning achievement of the rose world. Throughout the literature of roses are to be found tributes to this most elegant, most refined, most delicately beautiful and aristocratic of all roses. H.R. Darlington, one of England's greatest rosarians, wrote that 'the most beautiful forms in this group have perhaps most nearly attained perfection of form in the Rose'. The Rev. A. Foster-Melliar, of great reputation, called them 'the true aristocracy of the rose world'.

Alexander Hill Gray, a Scotman, was so desirous of growing them well that he sold up his property in Scotland and moved to Bath in order to grow them in a more suitable climate. I would have moved to France. Bath, though far more clement, is still a great deal too cold for these beauties. They found their ideal home in the warmer climes of the Mediterranean, in Australia, New Zealand, South Africa and the southernmost states of the USA. It is there that so many flower peacefully on, many past their hundredth birthday, in quiet old gardens, around colonial farmhouses still in use or abandoned, and marking old graves. Despite neglect, they flower continuously and beautifully, with as many as a thousand blooms in various stages at any one time. That such fragile elegant beauty should survive such extreme neglect is extraordinary. Many have known neither pruning nor fertilising in fifty years or more.

Yet in England and most of Europe the Tea roses had the reputation of extreme delicacy. Many certainly lack hardiness in great cold and each exceptionally bad European winter will take toll of the old plants there. Nevertheless many bushes have survived upwards of a century of cold to arctic winters. Frost protection, achieved by pruning back and wrapping in a protective layer of hay, oilskins or whatever, has permitted tea roses to be grown in places where winter temperatures may sink to 30° below zero. The huge collection in Sangerhausen in East Germany, for instance, survives regular bitter winter conditions with such treatment. Even if you live in the equivalent of northern England, judicious selection of varieties should allow you to grow some tea roses without any fuss.

To read almost any modern to reasonably modern author on the subject of old-fashioned roses, you might well be excused for believing that there had never been such a group as the Tea-scented roses. They are at best summarily dismissed by a comment to the effect that they were a rather **weakly** parent of the modern Hybrid Teas. My already high opinion of Mr Jack Harkness, the English rose breeder, is only boosted by his know-ledgeable summary of the group in his book *Roses*. Would that he might see those glories of the past, still glorious as his grandfather John Harkness recalled them, growing in our kinder climate.

The original *R.* × *odorata* varieties from which the race of Tea-scented China roses commenced were 'Hume's Blush Tea-scented China' and 'Parks' Yellow Tea-scented China'. Although these varieties are generally thought to be lost, in his book *My World of Old Roses* Trevor Griffith included a photograph of a rose under the name of 'Hume's Blush' which was supplied to him from Denmark. If this rose was truly named, then it is likewise alive and well at the old Rookwood Cemetery in Sydney on a nineteenth century grave. There is no mistaking the very unusual flushing pattern on the creamy petals of this double rose. The foliage, too, is identical, and the scent a true tea scent. With photograph in one hand, rose in the other, they might well be twins. One must hasten to add, however, that Redouté's portrait is not so like. The rose at Rookwood has a growth pattern that one would expect to have come from a *R. gigantea* parent. 'Parks' Yellow Tea-scented China' remains lost to date, but who can say if it will not yet be found again in these kinder climes.

Somewhere in the vicinity of 1400 Tea roses were introduced and bred for nearly a century. Not all of these, of course, were to find their way to the various warmer colonial countries of the nineteenth century. Nevertheless the identification of Tea roses still growing in Australia is a daunting one indeed. Old catalogues and old books are of relatively little assistance. Witness the number of descriptions of white roses with a pink blush or the even more descriptions of creamy pink teas. They number in the hundreds and rarely is information provided on flower shape, stamen colour, leaf characteristics, and stipule and sepal characteristics. Only by careful comparison with the remaining overseas reference collections is it possible to be sure of the identification of many Tea Roses and this is being done little by little. Illustrations in old books can sometimes clinch an argument, as can spontaneous (ie. unprompted!) recognition by those old enough to remember them from childhood gardens.

In the meantime all the worthy surviving old Teas should, I believe, be re-entered onto the lists of specialist growers. With or without a name, they remain just as beautiful and it is vital that they be redistributed. As with some of the stubbornly nameless roses rediscovered in England, they should if necessary be renamed for distribution. In some instances, they may well be the last represen-tative of a famous name and, as such, in the greatest danger of extinction unless entered back onto commercial lists. Would 'Sophie's Perpetual' (plate 55) or 'Flaxmoor Big Pink' or 'Surpassing Beauty of Woolverstone' be less beautiful if we knew their older names? Is 'Fantin Latour' any less glorious if its original name is never known with certainty as 'Celine', or 'Sissinghurst Castle' less sumptuous under that name rather than its original.

What really matters is that these glorious roses of the past have been restored to a new generation of rose lovers. For the same reason, the quite possibly never-to-be-identified-with-certainty earlier Tea roses found in Australia should be entered with dispatch onto commercial lists. Those who redis-cover such roses will in some small way enter into the recorded history of the rose and will earn the thanks of all lovers of the older roses. And while the rose survives, the possibility of it being eventually identified also exists.

The tea roses are a distinctive group. In form an open and rather twiggy shrub which may with age achieve as much as three metres or more in height and as much in width, they are covered in hundreds of rose blooms at a time, blooming all year round. Not that those dimensions should frighten the reader. Judicious and gentle pruning will keep the Tea rose well within bounds. The leaves are smooth, shining and soft-textured when young, ovate, pointed and finely serrated. New growth is usually deep crimson and often curiously reduced during periods of rapid growth, making additional width with time. The peduncle tends to be weak for the weight of the flower, which results in the nodding head so charmingly characteristic of the Tea rose. Another point of distinction is the frag-rance, once identified never mistaken. Other characteristics include a round or depressed hep and, particularly in the early teas, semi-transparent petals which are always in Tea roses, of most delicate colourings and exquisite blendings, never harsh. The earlier Tea roses were in general semi-double, although by the 1870s and 1880s they were frequently fully double.

For so long the wondrous Tea roses have been threatened with total extinction. The ubiquitous Hybrid Teas, with all its demerits, had the value of novelty and the advantage of twentieth century mass promotion. They were far less susceptible to the very cold winters of northern Europe, which was enough to guarantee their dominance in the market, and the introduction of 'Soleil d'Or' into the breeding produced a dazzling new colour range which had novelty appeal. Never before had such scintillating reds, burning oranges and hot pinks ever been seen. They were also indisputably better florists' roses, with strong necks and much thicker petals.

But in warmer climates, in tranquil country gardens and old city ones, the Teas bloomed on and on, and their owners, undisturbed by any notion of keeping up with the Jones, were perfectly happy to accept their beauty and bounty. They are, for many collectors, the most loved of all the old roses and most worthy of restoration.

A surprising number of old Tea roses have now

been saved from old places in New Zealand and Australia. They are relatively easy to grow from semi-ripe cuttings, although budding is safer as some varieties are surprisingly difficult to establish by cutting, usually those that are rarest or most exciting!

All of the roses listed below have been found and are either currently available again through specialist nurseries in Australia and New Zealand or will be in the near future.

'Adam' (1833) One of the first Tea roses and certainly the first to make the world sit up and take notice of this glorious new class of roses. This is a strong growing Tea that is often treated as a pillar rose, reaching 4 m in height. It is fully double, large, flat when opened with a 'starred' centre, filled with fragrant creamy peach pink short petals with slightly rosier reverse. The buds are globular and in blushed-peach. Raised by Adam of Rheims.

'Anna Olivier' (1872) A full-petalled large-flowered Tea of creamy apricot-buff flushed with rose pink and with typical nodding head. The fragrance is lovely.

'Baronne Henriette de Snoy' (1897) (plate 84) A luscious creation, a large full-petalled bloom of creamy pink with slightly deeper pink reverse. 'Gloire de Dijon' was one of its parents and 'Madame Lombard' purportedly the other. It certainly has the former in its lovely full flower, and is both vigorous (to nearly 2 m) and very free-flowering.

'Bon Silène' (1839) Bred by Mr. Eugène Hardy, the then curator of the Luxembourg Gardens in Paris, to whom we are also indebted for the lovely damask 'Mme Hardy' and the extraordinary *R.* × *hulthemia hardii*. The well-formed blooms are a lively rose pink with golden shanks, which creates a glowing gay rose. The reverse of the petals, like the bud, is a deeper carmine pink. It is fairly double and the upright petals retain the cupped shape of the rose on opening. A vigorous and very free-flowering rose.

'Catherine Mermet' (1869) This rose was bred by Guillot and was destined to become one of the great florist Teas for glass-house forcing, even into the twentieth century. It is a full pale pink rose with creamy yellow bases to the petals which lends a faint golden glow. A faint flush of lavender sometimes occurs. It pales with ageing of the flower. It is still a beautiful rose with long pointed buds and a high-centred flower which make it an ideal forcing rose. It gave rise to many sports valuable to the floristry industry including 'The Bride', 'The Bridesmaid', and 'Muriel Graham', a pale cream faintly flushed with pink.'

'Contesse de Nadillac' (1871) This extremely lovely old Tea rose bred by Guillot has globular blooms of light apricot pink, the outer petals tending to pale coppery yellow. It was rated one of the great exhibition Teas and responds to a little pampering. Give it shelter from cold strong winds, feed it with compost and accept its gratitude.

'Comtesse Riza du Parc' (1876) William Paul described it as 'flowers salmon-rose tinted with copper; large, full and globular'. Very floriferous and tea-fragrant.

'Devoniensis' (1841) This is the nearest thing to clotted cream in a rose! The big creamy-white flat rose is stuffed with thick velvety petals and is quartered, although not precisely so, and slightly flushed in the centre. It has warm rich fragrance, and is a lovely, vigorous, free-blooming rose worthy of any garden. It was also known as the 'Magnolia Rose' and was raised in Devon. Despite various published claims to the contrary, it is anything but extinct!

'Duchesse de Brabant' ('Comtesse de Lambarthe', 'Countess Bertha') (1857) Indisputably one of the most beautiful roses ever bred. The flowers borne singly or in small clusters are cupped and each shell-like translucent petal is a blend of pure tender pinks with a pearl-like sheen. These flowers glow in a way no pink rose bred before or since ever has. The fragrance is a refreshing and delicious blend of wild rose and tea scent. The whole impression is of delicacy, purity and glowing colour and it belongs with cucumber sandwiches and lace tablecloths in the sunny parlours of yesteryear. This rose flowers endlessly, each flush completely smothering the bush, even in winter.

'Etoile de Lyon' (1881) A luscious very double, large clear yellow tea rose, so full as to have a six pointed star of folds rather than quartering and very fragrant. It is shaded with richer yellow in the centre and the head, despite its weight, is held very erect on long brownish-red stems. The young leaves are handsome, a deep reddish green. It is one of the colonial survivors of America, New Zealand and Australia.'

'François Dubreuil' The only pure true deep velvety red Tea rose that I know of and the abundantly fully double blooms are stunningly scented. This is a treasure deserving of dissemination to as many gardens as possible.

'General Gallieni' (1899) An extraordinarily coloured, cupped and quartered Tea rose responding quite remarkably to temperature changes. It is never the same twice running. Sometimes it is cream overlaid with strawberry pink, other times it is, one is quite sure, raspberry pink. Then to compound the issue it develops coppery reds and deep dark crimsons. A strong grower, smothering in its luscious confections.

'General Schlablikine' (1878) Sometimes classified as a Hybrid China, this is a very double rose of less than perfect form, its petals reflexing and the general form rather more 'starry' than quartered when fully opened. The colouring is rich and reward-ing, a buff and salmon mixture flushed with coppery and rosy red and it found favour with many gardeners for its excellent performance, floriferousness and colour. It is still a gay, good and lovable rose. I'm inclined to side with Hybrid China classifiers. The rose certainly favours its China ancestry.

'Grace Darling' (1884) The parentage of this exquisite rose is unsure and it was released as a Tea rose, although many now declare it a Hybrid Tea. If so, it strongly favours the Tea side of its ancestry. Grace Darling, the heroine who captured the imagination of the Victorians and became a household name not only then but for decades to come, lent her name and fame to this rose which could not help but succeed. But it is in its own right a lovely rose, very free-flowering, large and double with an exquisite blend of creamy white, pink, and delicate flushings of deeper pink with just a hint of buff-gold in its depths, gradually fading to near white. A rose of great refinement and worth.

'Hugo Roller' (plate 78) Few roses so epitomise the old cottages of the Hawkesbury district. Sometimes the cottage is long gone but Hugo flowers on and on in its glory. The flowers are very large, very full, creamy white beautifully shaded at the edges of the petals with drifts of ruby. The fragrance too is delicious and true. Older bushes may carry hundreds of blooms at a time. One of the finest garden Teas.

'Isabella Sprunt' (1865) This was a sport of 'Safrano' discovered by Rev. J.M. Sprunt and named for his daughter. It was an extraordinarily successful rose in its day with the same form as the parent but in a clear light yellow. It occasionally sports back to the parent on one branch.

'Jean Ducher' Surely one of the loveliest of an exceedingly beautiful class of roses. It elicits endless admiration in our gardens and rightly so. The double saucer-shaped very fragrant blooms are an exquisite peaches and cream mixture with an apricot glow, an indescribably beautiful creamy concoction. To my mind it is by far the best of the tea roses for large pots, forming a neat lowish spreading shrub.

'Lady Hillingdon' (1910) Elegant long copper-apricot buds unfurl to a luscious warm apricot double cupped flower which is tulip-shaped. The new foliage is a luscious deep coppery-crimson. In the morning and on cool days it is richly scented of ripe apricots, later deliciously fruity tea-scented. It is one of the richest yet most delicately coloured roses ever bred and is continuously in flower until mid-winter, when it takes a short holiday with us. Constance Spry said of it, 'The warm apricot of her flowers is well foiled by the rich colour of leaf and stem and the tea scent is delicious'; while Peter Beales called her 'one of the most distinguished survivors from Edwardian Society'.

'Lady Roberts' (1902) This rose occurred as a sport of 'Anna Olivier' and has long buds opening to full nodding fragrant blooms in a lovely blend of colours, rich apricot-orange overlaid with copper and crimson.

'Madame Antoine Mari' (1901) One of the loveliest of all Tea confections, with elegant strawberry-blushed buds unfurling to exquisite pale creamy large full blooms with a faint buff shading toward the centre, the lovely drifts of strawberry being retained on the backs of the outermost rows of petals. Recently discovered among the Rookwood roses. A lovely colour plate taken by G.S.Thomas is to be found in the recent reprint of *Roses for English Gardens* by Jekyll and Mawley.

'Madame Berkeley' (1899) This exquisite rose was redis-covered by Mr L. Wyatt in England, one of his many redis-coveries for which lovers of old roses must be grateful. She has exquisite exhibition form with high-centred buds, the guard petals reflexing back from the fairly full centres, and is a lovely salmon pink with a warm golden glow in the depths of the rose and crimson flushing around the edges of the outer metals. Very free-flowering.

'Madame Bravy' ('Danzille', 'Alba Rosea', 'Mme de Serfot', 'Mme Denis', 'Josephine Meltot') (1846) This was a famous Tea bred by Guillot with globular flowers in which the outer petals were somewhat short and the inner petals short and folded. The colour is creamy white delicately blushed with rosy pink and has that glistening effect so beautiful too in 'Duchesse de Brabant'. This rose was also famous as a parent of the first H.T. 'La France'.

'Mme Charles' *See* 'Old Climbing and Rambling Roses'.

'Madame Jules Gravereaux' (1901) This exquisite climbing Tea is still a rose to evoke memories. From exquisitely unfurling buds in clusters upon perfect high-pointed double blooms in old gold and cream with a touch of salmon, set off to perfection by plentiful dark foliage. Not in general at all cold sensitive. One of

the favourite Edwardian roses, certainly in England, surely still somewhere in Australia where it was once so loved.

'Madame Lombard' ('Mme Lambard') (1877) Amongst the finest of all Tea roses with salmon pink large, full, globular blooms shaded with buff and blushed with rose. An exquisite rose of perfect form much praised by Gertrude Jekyll.

'Madame de Tartas' (1859) A large fragrant rosy pink double bloom on a very strong shrub, this rose was in colonial Australia and New Zealand soon after its release, where it thrived and produced abundantly. It has a fantastic breeding record, being a parent of 'Mme Caroline Testout' and 'Marie van Houtte', and suspected by Jack Harkness of being the pollen parent of 'Mermaid'.

'Madame de Watteville' This dainty and modest rose has creamy, deeply cupped, full-petalled, very fragrant blooms that are edged with a fine thin line of carmine pink. The bush is relatively low-growing. It was considered one of the best Tea roses for growing under glass, although it needs no such assistance here. It's a luscious rose to combine with English lavender.

'Mlle Franziska Kruger' (1880) Certainly rescued in the United States and due for importation if not soon found in Australia—but surely it must be here, somewhere? Mademoiselle is similar in form to 'Etoile de Lyon' with very full flat blooms with a 'star' of petal folds in the centre, and as richly coloured as a sunset, in fawns, copper, yellow, peach, and lilac. The full heavy blooms nod on their brown stems.

'Maman Cochet' (1893) (plate 39) Bred by S. Cochet, this excellent Tea rose was generally considered to be one of the best ever bred. It is a fine large, high-centred, full-petalled rose of impeccable form, pale pink with just a hint of lilac in it giving it an old fashioned look, and shaded with rose. In the way of teas, it can sometimes be creamy-pink to cream. It was considered 'the Elite of the Rose Garden' in its day and remains a true aristocrat. Excellent for cutting.

'Marie van Houtte' (1871) 'Safrano' was its grandparent, 'Mme de Tartas' and 'Mme Falcot' the parents, and they should all have been proud of Marie. She is fragrant, large-flowered, very double with a fairly high centre, creamy yellow with drifts of carmine pink down the backs of, and edging, the petals. A strong rose, she is one of the major survivors of colonial gardens around the world.

'Minnie Francis' (1905) This is a strong Tea with large high-centred blooms with that characteristic 'break' in the centre of the unfurling bud which I personally find endearing—perfection never has quite the appeal of a little frailty—in a rich medium pink. It ends up floppy and loose-petalled.

'Monsieur Tillier' (1891) (plate 3) In many ways this is an extraordinary Tea. The flowers are cupped, very full of short petals, the outer petals shell-like to form the cup, the inner petals folded. The colour almost defies description, a glowing rich pink washed with tea, with a coppery silken glow. The whole effect is rich and subtle, a colour infused with light. The fragrance is equally rich, of true Tea. The bush is very vigorous, very floriferous and almost never without flower, other than for a short rest at the end of winter. Controversy rages as to whether this is in fact 'Archduke Joseph' but old Australian catalogues support the name 'Monsieur Tillier'.

'Dr Grill' (1886) A superb Tea with large very full creamy blooms lightly blushed pink toward the edges and filled with true sweet tea fragrance. A very vigorous and trouble-free rose.

'Mrs B.R. Cant' (1901)   Big beautiful cupped blooms very full of petals and fragrance, a rich rose in colour merging to silvery rose in the centre and shaded buff at the base of the petals. Vigorous, trouble-free and floriferous.

'Mrs Dudley Cross' (1907)   Large perfectly formed creamy yellow blooms with delicate pink washes on the petals, that give rise to very pleasant arguments on the exact nature of fragrance. It reminds some of strawberries, others of bananas and still others of a delicious fruity tea mixture. Vigorous, almost thornless.

'Mrs Foley-Hobbs' (1910)   One of the last great Teas to be bred, with double fragrant blooms of excellent form in a light lemon yellow, blushed at the edges of the outer petals. An excellent healthy and desirable rose.

'Mrs Herbert Stevens' (1910)   Remembered with the greatest affection, this superb old Edwardian rose has the purest snow white perfectly formed high-centred blooms on long stems with the sweet fruity fragrance of freesias to many noses. It is vigorous, very floriferous and has light green foliage. It is by birth a Hybrid Tea, being the child of 'Niphetos' and the H.P. 'Frau Karl Druschki', but it strongly favours the tea side of its inheritance other than in its strong flower stalk, and is rightly grouped by most rosarians with the Teas. It has been a great florists' rose and a reliable source of income for the producer of field-grown winter roses, especially for winter weddings.

'Niphetos' (1843)   No more exquisite white rose, in bud or half open, has ever been bred. The long white buds are exquisite, opening through a tulip formation to a more or less double rose in which the central petals remain closed for some time over the centre, to create an effect often seen in double camellias. The flowers are large, shaded to pale lemon in the centre, and the papery white petals create a feeling of delicacy. Its name is Greek for 'snowy', and it was one of the great florists' roses so perfect for bridal bouquets and buttonholes. It was frequently called the 'Bridal Rose'. It was a great favourite of Constance Spry who wrote of it, 'How beautifully the grey-green reflexed calyx and soft colour of the leaves set off the fragility of the flowers; the petals are translucent and silken and the aristocratic head is richly heavy, bending down with its weight the slender stems'. One should add that it has sweet Tea fragrance, and that it is a frequent survivor at Rookwood in Sydney.

'Noella Nabonnand'   *See* the chapter 'Old Climbing and Rambling Roses'.

'Papa Gontier' (1883)   Surely one of the gayest roses ever bred, the large loosely double, cupped and nodding blooms seem to be made of crumpled rich rose silk, an improbable and delicious rose full of good cheer. The reverse of the petals and buds are just a shade deeper. Never without flower even in the depths of winter and very, very floriferous. It was one of the florists' roses, grown in glasshouses for forcing. How glad this splendid large rose must have been to escape its glass prison to the warmer climes of Australia.

'Penelope'   A very elegant Tea rose of Australian breeding with long creamy white and blushed buds opening to cream-white double blooms blushed at the edges with ruby red. A most sophisticated rose on a healthy medium-sized bush. A climbing form also exists.

'Perle des Jardins' (1874)   This was an incredibly popular rose in its day in Australia where late black frosts never malformed its summer blooms. These are very full, flat, fragrant and quartered, in a soft yellow shade, often blushed soft pink on the outside petals with a copper cast on the centre ones. This rose, unlike 'Etoile de Lyon', does nod on its stalk.

'Rosette Delizy' (1922)   This was one of the best of all the Tea roses, and has cadmium yellow double very fragrant blooms that are edged with bronzed-red. The whole plant is very vigorous and free-flowering.

'Safrano' (1839)   This was reputedly the first rose known to have been created by hand pollination and was raised by a M. Beauregard. The colour was perfectly described by William Paul: 'Flowers saffron to apricot in the bud, changing to pale buff'. The tea-fragrant flowers are semi-double with large loose petals opening from most elegant long buds. It was said in the nineteenth century that if one rose were flowering in the garden, it was sure to be 'Safrano'. It is still true. Even in the depths of winter here it is covered in bloom and the new shoots of spring may well carry about sixty blooms or more.

'Snowflake' ('Marie Lambert') (1886)   This lovely old Tea is reputedly a sport from the older rose 'Mme Bravy'. It is identical to the parent, fragrant, fully double with a pointed centre and cupped petals, in pure white.

'Sombrieul'   *See* the chapter 'Old Climbing and Rambling Roses'.

'Souvenir d'Elise Vardon' (1855)   A watershed rose, bred by Marest of Paris, this is a rose of exquisite beauty when well grown. 'Incomparable. Worthy of every care', purred the great Thomas Rivers. 'Nothing has been raised to surpass or even equal it', added Foster-Melliar. The flower form is much as we think of the Hybrid Tea with its high centre, the first rose to have this form which a later generation imagines to be traditional. It is a creamy salmon paling as it opens, a more rosy-salmon though still light on the backs of the petals.

'Souvenir de Madame Leonie Viennot' (1898)   What a lovely rose this is! Big, fairly full, saucer-shaped blooms that open creamy-yellow flushed with pink, the flushing deepening as the bloom ages revealing its China ancestry. It has an air of elegance and delicacy, and the blooms come throughout winter as well as every other month.

'Souvenir de Thérèse Levet'   One of those old roses that evokes sighs of memory and was a top seller at the end of the last century and the beginning of this. It has elegant nodding deep red buds overlaid with coppery-purple metallic sheen and the older petals of the blooms have this same curious wash on the petals. It is extremely prolific of blooms, almost weighed down by them.

'Souvenir d'un Ami' (1846)   (plate 5) A rose that inspires 'purple prose' from so many authors, perhaps because of its sturdy friendly reliability. It is a great colonial survivor in Australia, New Zealand, the USA and elsewhere, its cheery abundance of bloom marking the sites of many a long gone lonely farmhouse and cottage. With time it becomes quite a large shrub of 1.5 m– 2 m, smooth stemmed and almost thornless in young growth, bearing masses of perfectly circular, large, slightly cupped blooms of salmon and rose lit with an inner glow. It blooms deep into winter. Ethelyn Emery Keays bears quoting: 'Remarkable, as well, is the texture of the petals which are of the consistency, strength, and elastic softness of a non-crushable resillient dull silk we long for but never see. The colour is, likewise, exquisitely soft, being a light rose, deeper in the centre, with yellow shanks, so suffused with light or infused with colour that the effect is that of salmonish rose'. Even that phlegmatic Victorian gentleman William Paul called it 'very fine'.

'The Bride' (1885)   A very popular rose in its day, this was an exquisite white sport of 'Catherine Mermet'. It was released by H.B. May of New Jersey and was generally considered to be of better form than its parent. It was, as intended, a raging success with the wedding trade.

'The Bridesmaid' (1893)   Not yet restored to the lists, this is a clear pink sport of 'Catherine Mermet' which presumably was named to take that proportion of the wedding trade not already cornered by another 'Catherine Mermet' sport 'The Bride'. It was considered by many rosarians to be superior to Catherine and was released by the Moore Nursery in Tyler, Texas.

'White Duchesse de Brabant'   In all respects like its glorious pink mother, and presumably a sport from her. The colour is pearl white with the subtlest suffusion of fawn, almost a pale apricot-pink, in its depths. Its fragrance is utterly delicious as befits such a refined and glorious rose.

'White Maman Cochet' (1896)   This sport of its famous pink mother was to exceed her in fame, a rose of such excellence that it was generally recommended as the best white Tea of its day, with big, full, heavy white blooms of great substance and perfect form, borne prolifically on an excellent bush.

A Glory of Musks

I saw the sweetest flower wild nature yields,
A fresh blown musk-rose; 'twas the first that threw
Its sweets upon the summer: graceful it grew
As is the wand that Queen Titania wields.

John Keats (1795–1821)

A very special place is reserved in the rose world for a group of shrub roses that, by loosest connection might be said to be the children of that wild white rose of wanton fragrance, the Musk rose. They have in common lusty growth, an abandonment of blossoming rare even among the roses, rich fragrance, and most gracious and subtle colourings. They make ideal hedgerows, specimen plantings or glorious backdrops to the smaller roses. They are a special enchantment.

Most of the treasured Musk roses were bred by the Rev. Joseph H. Pemberton, a curate in Romford in Essex from 1880–1903. He eventually resigned his position as dioscesan inspector to grow roses. He bred a number of exquisite shrub roses, some of which were not released until after his death. It was fortunate indeed that they passed into the careful and skilled hands of his then gardener J.A. Bentall.

'Buff Beauty' (plate 51) (1939) has nodding heads of old gold roses shaded to buff filled with a sleepy, summery scent. The elegant spreading shrub is weighed down under its burden of bloom and it repeat flowers most reliably. It makes, in addition, one of the great weeping standing roses. It is one of the roses bred by the Rev. Pemberton released after his death.

'Cornelia' (plate 66) (1925) is almost never out of flower, bearing masses of small very fragrant, double flowers on long arching sprays. The coral pink buds open to reveal glowing pearl-sheened petals of delicate pink lit from within by a subtle gold glow. It is a uniquely beautiful rose, rarely out of flower and magnificent in spring and autumn.

Less well known is 'Thisbe' (1918), one of the loveliest little roses in the group. It is a small shrub bearing heads of small, semi-double, intensely fragrant champagne-coloured blooms. They are followed by tiny red heps.

'Felicia' (1928) is a compact bushy shrub to about 1.5 m in height. It resulted from a cross between 'Trier', the first of the Hybrid Musks, and the much loved old pink Hybrid Tea 'Ophelia'. The flowers are exquisitely shaped, richly fragrant, in a warm apricot-pink to silvery pink. It repeat flowers through to the end of autumn.

If ever there was a moonlight rose it is 'Prosperity' (1919). It was one of the Rev. Pemberton's exquisite creations and involved a cross between the great old Tea rose 'Perle des Jardins' and the Polyantha 'Marie-Jeanne'. 'Prosperity' is a rose of enormous charm forming an upright shrub to 1.5 m, smothering in sweetly fragrant ivory-white double blooms in clusters, followed by rich red medium-sized fruit contrasted against dark green foliage.

'Pax' is a rose for the larger garden. It forms a big lax rose with masses of drooping elegant creamy-white semi-double blooms in clusters. It has rich fragrance that is detectable at a distance.

For those who love the gay charm of the Polyantha, 'Ballerina' (1937) must appeal. It is a dear little shrub that clothes almost entirely in clear pink single little blooms with paler eyes. Another favourite of all those who love simple roses is 'Autumn Delight', with large scallops of almost single creamy-buff blooms that fade to creamy-white. Its fragrance is magnificent.

'Bishop Darlington' reminds me of a Tea rose with its elegant long peach-coloured buds opening to loosely informal, large semi-double, creamy white blooms. It has the true sweet original musk fragrance, and is almost never without flower.

Two delightfully cheery roses are 'Elmshorn' (1950) and 'Vanity' (1920). Some roses seem to be bred with joy in their hearts. 'Elmshorn' is one, an unmistakable shrub rose cascading with masses of small deep pink cheery silken pompons of sweetly fragrant blooms. It flowers magnificently in spring and autumn with little showers of blooms in between. 'Elmshorn' is very much a child's rose, to be picked and to shelter beneath.

'Vanity' (plate 94) is a tall-growing shrub, always leggy at the base and therefore best placed at the back of the border or underplanted. It was raised from a cross with that 1908 Hybrid Tea of 'darkest red, black as night', 'Chateau de Clos Vougeot'. 'Vanity' has large single blooms of bright rose pink silk with a lovely centre of golden stamens. It is exceedingly fragrant, to many reminiscent of the exquisite fragrance of old-fashioned sweet-peas. No description of the Musk Hybrids would be complete without the exquisite 'Penelope'. The large flowers borne in fragrant abundance are semi-double with slightly frilled edges, creamy pink with deeper flushings at the edges.

The Rose of Japan

The Ramanas Rose of Japan (*Rosa rugosa*) is actually native to Japan, China and Korea. It is in many ways the answer to a rose grower's prayers for it is almost indestructible. It grows happily, if necessary, in light sandy soils, is completely tolerant of salt laden winds, will take freezing conditions yet revels in our extremely hot summers. Added to all these virtues is a total indifference to mildew and black-spot. It is the ideal rose for the organic gardener for no sprays are ever required (although apart from using under-plantings of herbs, garlic spray and plenty of manure, we use nothing on any of our old roses)

Many of the varieties are amongst the best of all the hedging roses and I would defy a goat to pass through. Any other virtues? The heps produced only by the single and semi-double varieties, are huge, like glowing red tomatoes giving a fantastic display and mingling with bloom until the end of autumn. The heps are very richly endowed with vitamin C and make a valuable syrup. If that is not enough they have the most delicious fragrance, reminiscent of the old rose perfumes mixed with the spicy clove overtones of the clove pinks. They are in continuous flower until the end of autumn. The foliage is also excellent, with glorious autumn colouring. You will gather that I do like the Rugosa roses.

One of the most exquisite of all these roses is *R. rugosa alba* (plates 19 and 89). It has huge saucer-shaped, single, pure white blooms of lovely spicy fragrance, accentuated by a cluster of golden stamens, marvellous dark green foliage and the customary huge red heps.

R. rugosa typica has largish flowers of lilac pink, fragrant, and followed by luscious red heps. The seed comes reasonably true and if you have patience, time and a sandy bank to stabilise, you could do much worse than planting it up with seedling Rugosa Typicas. *R. rugosa rubra* is a deeper, richer, claret-coloured, large-flowered form with contrasting yellow stamens. There are many inferior forms of 'Rubra', all recognisably strains of this variety.

One of my own favourite Rugosa Hybrids is 'Mme George Bruant' (1887). What a delicious marriage between a Rugosa and a Tea rose! The creamy white buds open to big fragrant, floppy, semi-double pure white flowers with lemon-gold stamens. The foliage resembles the Rugosa side of the parentage. It is very floriferous and recurrent. More double, like a very large, sweetly fragrant formal white camellia is 'Blanc Double de Coubert' (1892). In warm dry weather it is a most impressive shrub rose although the pure papery white petals will spoil in rainy weather. The blooms come with great freedom and constant succession however. Coubert, in case you have ever wondered, is the French village where the famous rose breeder Cochet-Cochet raised this rose. The parents were, as with 'Mme George Bruant', *R. rugosa* and a Tea rose, in this instance 'Sombrieul'. In 1899 a sport appeared of 'Blanc Double de Coubert' which was named 'Souvenir de Philemon Cochet'. It is very double and fragrant, with a deliciously crumpled centre of soft creamy pink and deserves to be much more widely grown. Somewhere in between is 'Schneezwerg' (1912) with lovely fragrant pure white semi-double flowers with a large boss of golden stamens, much resembling a large Japanese anemone. It flowers almost endlessly from spring to late autumn, and produces small orange heps. It is also sold under the name of 'Snow Dwarf'.

In the pale pink colours is to be found one of the most exquisite roses of any group, 'Frau Dagmar Hastrup' (plate 56) (also 'Frau Dagmar Hartropp'). The huge fragrant single saucer-shaped blooms are a delicate pink and look deceptively fragile. They are followed by equally huge glowing tomato-red heps. It is quite low-growing, certainly never more than medium sized, well clothed in good Rugosa-type foliage and an asset in any garden. Other rugosas that can easily be accommodated in the smaller garden are 'Belle Poitevine', 'Fimbriata' and 'Pink Grootendorst'.

The rose's genetic heritage seems to include a tendency to produce carnation-like fringing of the petals. The China rose, *R. chinesis serratipetala*, for instance, is quaintly serrated at the edges, and the Rugosa roses appear to have the same tendency. In 1891 'Fimbriata' was introduced, a very pretty rose of fragrant small palest pink to white frilled carnation-like blooms in clusters. It also went under the prettier names of 'Dianthiflora' and 'Phoebe's Frilled Pink'. It was raised, so the story goes, from a cross between *R. rugosa* and 'Mme Alfred Carriere', made by a M. Morlet of Avon in France. The Rugosas were to produce another frilly offspring in 1918, this time with clusters of red carnation-like blooms. It was raised by F.J. Grootendorst and Sons, of Boskoop, and released under their name. It was raised from a cross between *R. rugosa rubra* and 'Mme Norbert Levavasseur', a Polyantha. A lovely clear pink sport with the same frilly petals, introduced in 1923, was called 'Pink Grootendorst', while 'Grootendorst Supreme' (1936) is a darker red sport. These are all upright growing medium height shrubs of mildly spreading habit.

'Belle Poitevine' (1894) makes a restrained hedge or privacy screen to 1.5 m and covers in very beautiful semi-double floppy lilac pink blooms with creamy stamens.

For taller screening and hedging nothing could be more charming than 'Sarah Van Fleet' (1926). It is tall-growing and forms a dense spreading shrub. For hedging, plants should be spaced one metre apart, and pruned back each spring to 1.5 m to force new dense growth. It bears masses of large semi-double cupped blooms of clear pink, each with a central boss of creamy stamens. It is intensely fragrant and flowers repeatedly in heavy flushes of bloom from spring to late autumn. Added to all these virtues are light green glossy foliage and the ability to tolerate some shade. Nothing could be more desirable than to make a secret garden walled with this dense, deliciously fragrant pink hedging rose and to laze away soft summer days within its protection.

'Rose à Parfum de l'Hay' (1903) (plate 88) is one of the most loved of the Rugosa roses. It has large cherry-red globular blooms with a marvellous rich Damask scent and is considered by some to be the most fragrant rose of all. It forms a lowish-growing, spreading shrub. Equally successful in Australia is 'Roseraie de l'Hay' (1901), a superb specimen rose which will form a dense shrub 2.5 m high and wide, clothed to the ground with healthy green foliage. It bears masses of semi-double rich wine-red fragrant blooms in clusters, which open from elegantly furled buds. Should you prefer to create a walled garden of this sumptuous red rose, it will form an excellent large hedge or impenetrable screen in a couple of years, again planted to one metre apart and treated in the same way as 'Sarah Van Fleet'.

'Scabrosa' is another excellent hedging rose though not one for creating garden walls as it reaches only 1.5 m. It forms a superb hedge for the Royal National Rose Society's garden in England, where the main requirements were that the chosen rose should have foliage down to ground level and never fall victim to blackspot. It overcomes both these hurdles without faltering, to which should be added the virtues of rich violet crimson, crumpled single blooms that unfold in the sun to reveal large delicate fuchsia-pink petals, dusty stamens and sweet fragrance. The blooms are followed by fabulous huge tomato-red heps.

An old red Rugosa, 'Mrs Anthony Waterer' (1898) has wonderful globular, deep crimson, very fragrant blooms which are borne prolifically along its tall arching branches. It will comfortably reach two metres and should be reserved for the back of the rose border, or can be pegged down in the manner of the Hybrid Perpetuals.

Into the giant category come 'Conrad Ferdinand Meyer' (1899) and 'Lady Curzon' (1901). Conrad makes a huge spectacular spreading bush to three metres high or more with a breathtaking display of huge silvery-pink, semi-double, fragrant, floppy blooms of typical Edwardian opulence. Its only drawback is that with time it will get leggy and looks best underplanted as the years go by with smaller shrubs such as purple buddleias, with lavenders and cotton lavenders further to the front. 'Nova Zembla' (1907) is a pure white sport of 'Conrad' and richly scented. 'Lady Curzon' is on an equally grand scale reaching 2.5 metres or more if given a chance. The fragrant, almost single large blooms are a clear irridescent pink with a pale yellow centre and golden stamens. Unlike the great majority of Rugosa roses, there is only one blooming, but it lasts a long time and is absolutely superb.

One of only two yellow Rugosas ever bred is 'Agnes' (1922). It resulted from a cross with *R. foetida persiana* and is a strangely appealing rose with medium sized, very double pompons of pale amber yellow shading to cream around the edges, very sweetly scented. It is recurrent flowering although not as much as some. The bush is quite tall in time, to two metres or a little more and quite spreading with very good bright green ferny foliage. The appeal may well lie in the charmingly muddled form of the blooms, which is a characteristic I always find difficult to resist.

Collecting Rugosa roses can be quite a sizable challenge in its own right and a rewarding one. Others well worth collecting are: 'Carmen' (1907) with large rich crimson single fragrant blooms; 'Delicata' (1898) with big sweetly-scented, semi-double, cerise pink blooms, golden stamens and huge orange heps; and 'Calocarpa' (1895), perpetual blooming with big single purple-crimson blooms. 'Foliolosa' grows into an excellent well-rounded, well-clothed shrub with large velvety glowing crimson single blooms which are dusted in pollen from the golden stamens and are followed by clusters of big deep crimson, shining heps. Two delightful modern hybrids worthy of collection are

'Martin Frobisher' (plate 46) (1969) with deliciously fragrant, large, rich pink, double blooms opening from perfect plump buds, paling around the edges and revealing a crown of golden stamens; and the rare-coloured 'Dr Eckener' with fragrant, glowing peach pink, semi-double blooms with yellow centres. Both can grow to two metres.

In a family with such a wealth of virtues, a warning note must be struck over those Rugosas recommended as groundcovers. Without exception they are formidably vigorous, aggressive and martially thorned and I wouldn't personally plant one of them. Our warm climate promotes the kind of weed growth that makes me shudder at the thought of weeding between their thorny arms. They may be a greater success in highly managed gardens in cooler regions. They can still find a place, however, if used to cascade over brick or stone walls and embankments. In such a location their spreading growth and curtain of flowers can be very effective. Choose from 'Max Graf' (1919) with quite charming, large clear pink, fragrant single blooms with yellow stamens; *R.* × *paulii* with white single blooms; and *R.* × *paulii rosea* with, of course, pink blooms. All are once flowering, usually in late spring.

Pony or Baby Roses

Miniature roses have an appeal which is difficult to deny. In the garden they look well planted at the front of a border. I like to mix them with the low-growing form of English lavender, 'Munstead', which sprawls engagingly onto paved walkways, and old-fashioned clove pinks with spices in their throats. Dark blue forget-me-nots such as the alpine forget-me-not, the wild blue field forget-me-not and the dainty pink one look lovely too, as does the rich blue of alpine columbines, and the exquisite enchantment of Victoriana columbines. Tiny bulbs such as Canaliculata, the hoop daffodil, snowflakes and snowdrops, the wood anemones blend charmingly. Dwarf fuchsias, particularly some of the nineteenth century dwarf forms, are very appropriate as a background. The dwarf white lavender and the pink lavender make old-fashioned interplantings with the taller white lavender, with its silvery foliage, and English lavender in the background. If all else fails, these delightful Baby roses will grow well in large pots.

The oldest of all our tiny roses come from the Centifolia family. These appeared in the seventeenth century and continue to enchant generation after generation of gardeners. They became particularly associated with children by the unashamedly sentimental Victorians who gave them to children for their own gardens. Thomas Rivers (1854) said that children of that time loved the Dwarf Provence roses and called them affectionately Pony or Baby roses. They were grown on their own roots by cutting or layering, and customarily used as an edging to their small gardens. In France, where the art of pot-grown flowers as part of the florist's trade has long flourished, the Dwarf Provence roses provided a profitable and long-lasting fashion. Fine English china originating from the nineteenth century was often hand-painted with these charming roses.

Perhaps the best known of the Baby roses is 'De Meaux' which sat for its portrait by Redouté at Malmaison under the title of *R. pomponia*. This little treasure is almost an exact miniaturisation of the 'Rose des Peintres', with exquisite small pink pompon blooms no more than 25 mm across, filled with delicious sweet fragrance. The foliage is miniature too. It is thought to have been named for the flower-loving Bishop of Meaux, Domenique Seguier. A white form of 'De Meaux' also exists, actually a flower of palest blush fading to white.

A mossy form of 'De Meaux' appeared in 1814 in a garden at Taunton in Somerset and was eagerly acquired by a Mr Sweet of the Bristol Nursery. 'Moss de Meaux' was 'very small, the earliest of roses, blooms in clusters of a delicate pink colour'. It was said that he acquired this desirable Baby rose for the sum of five pounds, later releasing it at one guinea each. He was undoubtedly a man with an eye for a rose and its value and it is a matter for regret that this beautiful little rose may have been lost, although another Baby Moss rose, 'Little Gem' (1880), has been reintroduced in England. It has small, light crimson, very fragrant pompon blooms with ample green mossing tinged with pink.

The Burgundy rose was first found in Burgundy in 1664 and is now thought to be a sport of the common cabbage rose. It was illustrated, like royalty, by all the finest artists of its long life: Redouté, Parsons and Andrews, for instance, all paid it their highest honours. It is a mere 0.5 m in height, if that, with perfect, very compact, dark tyrian pink blooms suffused with claret, filled with lovely scent, no more than 25 mm across. It acquired various names in its travels including 'Parvifolia', 'Pompon de Bourgogne' and 'Pompon de Rheims'. Slightly deeper in colour is 'Pompon de Saint François'.

'Petite de Hollande' is a Baby rose of unknown date of origin. It went under other names such as

'Petite Junon de Hollande', 'Pompon des Dames' and 'Normandica' and was on sale in England in 1770. It may well be one of the very old seventeenth century Dutch Centifolias. It is in any case a charming fragrant Centifolia covering itself with small soft pink, cupped flowers filled with shorter petals and blushed deeper. In a delightful group, this is one of the most desirable, growing to one metre in height with arching canes.

'Spong' (plate 79) (1805) grows to no more than one metre, covering itself in fragrant, rich deep pink, cupped blooms borne uprightly on a compact plant. Its unlikely name is due to the gardener who introduced it, and C.C. Hurst identifies it with a rose mentioned in 1789 under a name which defies sane comment, 'The Great Dwarf Rose'.

The China roses were, in their turn, to provide many new Baby roses for the delight of nineteenth century gardens. Many of these miniature treasures are still with us today, each worthy of a place in the modern garden. The Chinas are very repeat blooming. It is almost impossible not to find the odd flower even in the depths of winter.

'Anna Maria de Montravel' (1880) is an exquisite rose, of compact growth to 1 m with airy double, cupped, pure white blooms in fragrant clusters. It blooms prolifically. 'Little White Pet' (plate 62) (1879) which has also acquired the name of 'Belle de Teheran' is very free-flowering with clusters of little double creamy white pompon flowers that open from blushed pink buds. It reaches around 0.7 m in height and is complemented by dark glossy green foliage. It has been suggested that it is a dwarf recurrent flowering form of the old rambler rose 'Felicite et Perpetue', but is usually placed with the Chinas.

'Hermosa' (1840), sometimes written 'Armosa' and having acquired the additional names of 'Melanie Lemaire' and 'Mme Neumann', is usually classed with the China roses, but it has a great deal of the Bourbon rose about it. It must be one of the most loved and desired of all the Baby roses, with clusters of globular, intensely fragrant, soft clear pink blooms with just a hint of lilac, set off by blue-green foliage. The compact little shrub reaches no more than one metre in height and owes its great and endless freedom of bloom to its China ancestry.

'Mignonette' (1880) is very free-flowering on a small shrub rarely more than 0.5 m in height, clothed with light green foliage. It smothers in repeated blooming of small double, soft rosy pink blooms in clusters and, as with 'Little White Pet', makes a wonderful edging to a path.

'Echo' (1914) or 'Baby Tausendschön' (Baby Thousand Beauties Rose) makes a compact bushy shrub to one metre high, smothering in cupped semi-double blooms of pink which fade delightfully through a subtle mixture of pinks to white. All the different colours are on the bush at once to create an exquisite effect like old brocade.

For those who love the effect of deep crimsons and rich velvety reds, the Chinas offer three little roses that are almost never without bloom. 'Fabvier' (1832) is a scarlet-crimson beauty reaching only 0.5 in height or a little more, with dense twiggy growth, very free-flowering with cupped blooms occasionally sporting a fine white streak. 'Semperflorens' (1792), which is thought to be 'Slater's Crimson China', has fragrant flowers up to 50 mm across in a lovely velvety crimson. It grows a little taller than 'Fabvier'. The last of the trio, 'Cramoisi Supérieur' (plate 92) (1832) or 'Agrippina', is low-growing, spreading and very free-flowering, covering itself repeatedly with clusters of cupped semi-double, rich deep crimson blooms.

Not really a miniature, growing to about one metre in height but with baby 'flowers' perfect for miniature posies, is 'The Green Rose of China', or 'Viridiflora' (plate 81). It was introduced in 1743 and is formed of jade green petals attractively bronzed and rouged with age.

Everyone's favourite is 'Cecile Brunner' (plate 49) which was introduced by Pernet-Ducher of Lyon in 1881. The exquisite pink buds are thumbnail-sized copies of perfect icecream pink 'Ophelia' roses. It is supposedly a cross between a Tea rose and a Polyantha, so that it is a Hybrid China by closest definition. In England it was often known as 'The Sweetheart Rose', while in France it was called 'Mignon'. A climbing sport occurred in 1894, in California, very vigorous and a provider of many delightful buttonhole roses.

Another sport, despite the written records, is 'Bloomfield Abundance' (plate 57), to which 'Cecile Brunner' has been attested to sport by many nurserymen and field growers. This is sometimes known as the 'Shrub Cecile Brunner' and was released in 1920. The exquisite little blooms are identical except for the sepals which are much longer, foliacious, and far more elegant in 'Bloomfield Abundance'. This rose grows to approximately 2.5 m in height with huge airy panicles of fifty or more little roses each. It provides an abundance of fragrant buttonhole roses in spring and autumn with lighter flushes of bloom in between.

Two roses in the same style as 'Cecile Brunner', differing only in colour, are 'Mme Jules Thibaud', which is believed to be a sport of Cecile with a deeper peachy pink colour, and 'Perle d'Or' (1884), sometimes called 'Golden Cecile Brunner'. Far from being the modern golden yellow that many people expect, this rose is an exquisite old-gold to apricot-pink, depending on the temperature, paling to creamy apricot on opening and fragrant. The bud is the same as Cecile but differs on opening by being more double. A white sport of 'Cecile Brunner' called 'White Cecile Brunner' (1909) is identical to the parent other than in colour, the buds being cream and opening creamy white with a lemon touch to the centres and fragrant.

The infusion of *Rosa multiflora* blood into the Chinas created a new class of baby roses with clsuters of blooms, the Polyanthas. They were to give way to the larger-flowered Floribundas, but they created a class of charming roses some of which may still be had today. Roses of the true Polyantha persuasion are still occasionally produced and appeal greatly to those who know of their fairylike enchantment. One such rose, appropriately known as 'The Fairy' (1941), is a dear rose bearing endless flushes of tiny, exquisite, pale pink, silken flowers in large clusters. It entered the world with no ripple of promotion yet went on to win awards and hearts ever since. Equally exquisite is one of Jack Harkness' loveliest creations, 'Yesterday' (plate 17). If ever a rose was born out of time and out of space, it was this rose. It was released in 1974 but looks far more at home in 1874. It is an elegant little rose producing airy masses of semi-double rosy pink cupped blooms with yellow stamens aging to paler pink with a delicate hint of lavender, the mixture of colours on the one little shrub being sheer delight. To add to its many charms its fragrance is outstandingly sweet. Its ancestry includes 'Shepherd's Delight, 'Phyllis Bide' and 'Ballerina' and it is Jack Harkness' expressed hope that 'Yesterday' will lead the Polyanthas to their tomorrow.

'China Doll' (1945) is one of the gayest and most charming little Polyantha roses of this century. It is a bushy little shrub of glossy dark green to about 0.5 m carrying endless flushes of great rounded, bright rosy pink flower clusters that smother the little plant. The individual flowers are sweetly scented. It is the ideal little rose to border a path or garden.

Of the same cheerful and charming disposition is 'Orléans Rose' (1909) with slightly double, vivid rose pink blooms with a conspicuous white eye, borne in clusters. It is taller than 'China Doll', reaching perhaps one metre.

Four Australian polyanthas are most deserving of tribute and are being once more acclaimed. These are 'Gay Vista' with clusters of single pink blooms with bright white eyes, 'Honeyflow' with innocent milky white single blooms in clusters, 'Claret Cup' (plate 67) with fragrant wine-red blooms with striking white eyes, and 'Carabella' (plate 14) with all the simple charm of appleblossom which it resembles. They were all created by Mr Frank Riethmuller of Sydney. These roses have all the appeal of old-fashioned wildlings and may easily find their place in the cottage garden.

Despite the hectic promotion of the last few years which would appear to herald a brand new class of roses, the Miniature roses are a group which have been evolving through much of this century.

The marketing of flowering roses in pots would likewise impress as being a new phenomenon. Pots of flowering Baby Centifolias, Polyanthas, and Chinas were however the stock in trade of the European florist of the nineteenth century. The English, with perfectly straight faces, went so far as to advertise 'Teas in Pots'. One of the charming little miniatures offered in the nineteenth century was a rose now known as 'Rouletti', which, with the passing of the trade in miniatures in pots, was thought to be lost. But in 1918 a Swiss Army Medical Officer named Roulet saw plants growing in pots in the Swiss village of Onnens. He was told by the villagers that the rose was known to have been in the village for approximately a century. It was very dwarf with double pink flowers. It was obtained from the village by Henri Correvon, a plantsman of Geneva, who had heard of Roulet's discovery. He reintroduced this little rose under the name of *R. roulettii*. It was to become the foundation of the modern Miniature roses.

Two lovely older Miniature roses to look for are 'Pour Toi' (1946) bred by Pedro Dot and one of the most perfect miniatures ever raised, with tiny white double flowers touched with cream. It was to acquire different names in different countries including 'Para Ti', 'For You' and 'Wendy'. 'Cinderella' was bred by DeVink in 1952, one of the few rare crosses ever achieved with 'Cecile Brunner', the other parent being 'Peon' ('Tom Thumb'). It has palest pink, very double flowers on a tiny bush and is altogether a charming plant.

'Easter Morning' was bred by that most enthusiastic and successful breeder of Miniatures, Ralph S. Moore of California. It is one of the loveliest Miniatures bred to date, with roses like thimble-sized Hybrid Tea blooms and lovely glossy foliage.

So many exquisite little Miniatures are now emerging, repaying the discovery of 'Roulettii' and the patient breeding efforts that have been expended upon it. To Ralph Moore we owe a series of delightful new Miniature Moss roses, a tribute to his vision and patience. Using 'Golden Moss' crossed with a seedling of that great red rose 'Charles Mallerin', a rose called 'Mark Sullivan', an F_1 seedling of pure yellow, was achieved. Crossed with 'Rumba' it produced 'Goldmoss', a mossy floribunda. As a second breeding line, a cross was achieved between 'Pinocchio' and 'William Lobb', the old Moss rose. A seedling of this cross when mated with 'New Penny' produced the very first true Moss Miniature, 'Fairy Moss'. It is a red rose with lovely mossing. From these hybrids Ralph Moore has continued to forge exquisite little Miniature Mosses. My favourite must be 'Dresden Doll' with perfect semi-double, cupped, pale pink blooms filled with golden stamens and sweet fragrance and exquisitely mossed buds. 'Lemon Delight' has masses of soft green mossed buds opening to sweetly fragrant semi-double lemon yellow blooms with golden stamens. 'Toy Balloon' is an exquisite little red Miniature Moss.

1. *Rosa laevigata* (1759) (*see* page 19), the Cherokee rose. Also known as *R. sinica alba*, it was at Elizabeth Bay House by the 1840s

2. Roses tumble down the author's mountain garden. In the foreground 'Tea Rambler' (*see* page 70), in the background the climbing form of the old bourbon 'Souvenir de la Malmaison' (1843) (*see* page 31) and 'Fortuneana' (1850) (*see* page 18)

3. A magnificent old Tea rose known as 'Monsieur Tillier' (*see* page 38)

4. Perhaps the greatest of all the Centifolia roses (*see* page 17), a rose of unknown origin renamed in honour of the great French flower artist, 'Fantin Latour' (*see* page 28) is a magnificent sight in full flower

5. 'Souvenir D'un Ami' (*see* page 39) (1846) is a very strong old Tea rose that has survived in many Australian and New Zealand gardens. The rich lovely colouring and delicious fragrance earn it a place today

6. The Rugosa roses (*see* page 15) are the answer to seaside plantings and are wonderfully trouble free. *Rugosa* 'Typica' (*see* page 42) has huge single fragrant flowers from spring to autumn followed by huge edible glowing red heps

7. 'Mme Alfred Carrière' (1879) (see page 18) has full cupped milky-white blooms, often faintly blushed to pale pink, with an exquisite old rose fragrance. It flowers prolifically in late spring and in autumn with intermittent flushes. Like all the great Noisettes, it is a superbly strong and healthy climber

8. A glorious tangle of old-fashioned roses in a Blue Mountain's garden in NSW. The huge pink rose is 'Constance Spry' (see page 24).

9. These huge heps like glowing red pippins occur on all the single and semi-double Rugosa roses

10. *Rosa gigantea* (1888) (see page 21), one of the largest of all climbers, with huge milky white single fragrant roses. It repeat flowers and bears large crops of golden fruit. The foliage is Tea-like

11. 'Félicité Parmentier' (1836) (see page 27) is a smaller-growing Alba with the most bewitching creamy-pink, very double flowers opening from plump rosy buds, richly fragrant of honeysuckle

12. Grand old Hybrid Perpetual 'Baron Giraud de l'Ain' (1897) has huge cupped rich red flowers deckle-edged with white. It is richly fragrant and very floriferous

13. The Noisette roses are unbelievably generous. Here 'Cloth of Gold' (1843) (*see* page 67) flowers late in May in David Ruston's garden at Renmark

14. 'Carabella' (*see* page 47), a Polyantha bred by Riethmuller of Sydney and released by the late and lamented Hazelwood's Nursery. This rose has all the innocence and charm of appleblossom and brings spring into the heart of the hottest mid-summer day

15. 'Crépuscule' (1904) (*see* page 67) is a very popular Noisette bearing masses of semi-double very fragrant flowers in a wonderful rare shade of apricot and old gold. It blooms repeatedly into early winter for us

16. 'Celsiana' (prior to 1750) (*see* page 26). One of the most breath-takingly beautiful and fragrant old roses, this Damask to 1.5 m is superb in every way with large fragile creamy-pink flowers delicately flushed deeper pink

17. 'Yesterday' (*see* page 47), A Polyantha-style rose bred by Harkness, forms a sturdy little bush to 1.2 m with masses of thimble-sized slightly double rich pink, lightly but sweetly scented flowers

18. The exquisite eglantine rose of Shakespeare (*R. eglanteria, see* page 13), with foliage which releases at the slightest touch the fragrance of ripe apples

19. Clove fragrant and exquisite Rugosa 'Alba' (*see* page 42)

20. 'Président de Sèze' (*see* page 23) ('Mme Hébert') is a glorious Gallica from prior to 1836, laden down in early summer with rosy pink buds that open to rich pink double blooms frosted to pale lavender at the edges

21. The 'Himalayan Musk Rose', *R. brunonii (see* page 20), is a vigorous and spectacular rambler to 7.5 m with clusters of delicate single creamy white, lightly scented blooms and light grey-green downy drooping leaves

22. 'Albertine' (1921), one of the greatest rambler roses, with masses of warm coppery-chamois to soft pink, informal, richly perfumed roses that here mingle with 'Wedding Day'

23. With the look of a wild rose, the exquisite large single blooms of the shrub rose 'Sparrieshoop' come from mid-spring to autumn

24. Nominated by Peter Beales at the 2nd International Heritage Rose Conference as his current favourite old rose, 'Narrow Water' originated in Ireland *c.* 1883 and grows to around 2.5 m high. This restrained rambler has a lovely scent

25. ''Düsterlöhe', descended from the Field rose (*R. arvensis*) (*see* page 20) has exquisite single cupped blooms of rich pure pink paling delicately at the edges, followed by large orange-red oval heps

26. 'Wedding Day', one of the finest first cousins of the climbing wild roses, was raised by Sir Frederick Stern at 'Highdown' in Sussex. A glory of a rose, richly fragrant of orange blossom and very vigorous

27. There are few climbing Hybrid Perpetuals but 'Mme Grégoire Staechlin' (*see* page 70) ('Spanish Beauty') is one. The well-shaped buds open to huge-semi-double clear pink blooms with deeper pink reverse and delicious sweet-pea fragrance

28. 'Donna Maria', an exquisite old Sempervirens Hybrid climber which smothers in small double white blooms. This beautiful specimen was grown by Deane Ross

29. One of our favourite shrub roses, 'Moonsprite', blends to perfection with the old roses

30. 'Mme Lauriol de Barny', a Bourbon from 1868, is a glorious French rose to 1.5 m or more, the arching canes covering in silvery pink very fragrant large quartered blooms

31. 'Gloire Lyonnaise' from 1885, a huge cupped pure white hybrid perpetual with sweet fragrance, reliably repeat flowering into late autumn

32. 'Rose d'Amour' ('St Mark's Rose'), *R. virginiana plena* (*see* page 16). This lovely double-flowered hybrid was introduced into England in 1768. In Venice, it was expected to flower on the saint's day, 25 April

33. The Chestnut rose, *R. roxburghii plena* (1814) is a handsome rose from China which forms large bristly heps like the seedcases of chestnuts. The unusual foliage is equally handsome

34. 'Ispahan' (*see* page 25), a Damask dating to before 1832, with numberless clusters of double, clear rose-pink blooms of intense old rose fragrance. One of the roses extensively grown for the extraction of attar of roses for the perfumery industry

35. 'Leda' (*see* page 26), the painted Damask, dates back to prior to 1827. It is a very fragrant and distinctive old rose, the milky white petals looking as though they had been dipped into a pot of carmine rouge

36. One of the glories of the rose world, the old Noisette 'Lamarque' (*see* page 66), from 1830, which smothers in great swathes of large double white, very fragrant blooms in clusters. Few roses evoke fragrant moonlit nights as does 'Lamarque'

37. One of the prettiest of all old roses with plump-winged rosy buds in masses opening to very full fragrant blooms of creamy-pink, 'Belle Isis' (c. 1845) (see page 23) is ideal for the smaller garden

38. 'Tea Rambler' (1904) (see page 70), with full fragrant blooms which smother the plant in great powder puffs of rosy salmon, and a warm sweet Tea scent

39. 'Maman Cochet' (1893) (see page 38) was an amazingly successful rose in Australia. It was considered 'the elite of the rose garden' in its day

40. 'New Dawn' (1930) (see page 73) was a sport of the universally popular 'Dr W. van Fleet', and is a climbing rose of the most exquisitely delicate pale pink and sweetness of fragrance

41. 'Bourbon Queen' ('Reine de l'Isle Bourbon'), 1835, is best treated as a Pillar rose and is sweetly scented

42. 'Vivid' (1853), a very floriferous fragrant Bourbon of excellent habits

43. 'Shot Silk' (1931), both in its bush and climbing forms, has become a collector's item, with its silky glowing colours and delicious intense fragrance

44. 'Rosa Mundi' (*see* page 33) is an ancient Gallica, dating to prior to 1580, named for King Henry II's mistress, the fair Rosamund, daughter of Sir William de Clifford

45. 'Frühlingsgold' (*see* page 14), a Hybrid Spinosissima (recently changed to Hybrid Pimpinellifolia), a magnificent and fragrant specimen shrub

46. A Rugosa rose of more recent introduction, 'Martin Frobisher' (*see* page 44) has roses, exquisite at every stage, and very fragrant, smothering a big but neat specimen shrub to 2 m

47. 'Mme Pierre Oger' (*see* page 32), a Bourbon from 1878, is the epitome of old-fashioned roses, very sweetly scented, composed of shell-like petals in a warm creamy pink touched with rose

48. 'Celine Forestier' (*see* page 67), a Noisette from 1842, has a delicious spicy Tea fragrance and vigorous, fully remontant habit once established

49. 'Cecile Brunner' ('The Sweetheart Rose', 'Mignon') (*see* page 46) from 1881 still captures many hearts with its thimble-sized blooms like exquisite miniature 'Ophelia' flowers

50. 'Highdownensis' is a form of the climbing species rose *R. moyesii*. The spring flowering is followed by a wonderful display of orange-red flagon-shaped heps

51. 'Buff Beauty' (*see* page 40) with its exquisite nodding old gold heads of roses filled with sleepy summery scent was raised by the Rev. Joseph Pemberton

52. Exquisite 'Gruss An Aachen' from 1909, used by Major Lawrence Johnston at 'Hidcote' for the white garden

53. The 'Red Rose of Lancaster' (*see* page 22) (*R. gallica officinalis*), an ancient Gallica

54. Large and very beautiful single flowers smother the oddly-named Gallica Hybrid 'complicata' (*see* page 24), a shrub rose to 1.9 m

55. 'Sophie's Perpetual' (*see* page 36), a superb old China rose with fragrant cupped double blooms in quantity on a tall almost thornless bush. Discovered by Humphrey Brooke and reintroduced under a new name, it has already mutated to 'Sophe Perpetual'!

56. 'Frau Dagmar Hastrup' (*see* page 42), perhaps the most exquisite of all Rugosa roses

57. 'Bloomfield Abundance' (*see* page 46) ('Shrub Cecile Brunner') (1920), is a graceful tall arching shrub bearing huge airy panicles of 'Cecile Brunner' look-alike roses

58. 'Autumnalis' (*see* page 66) is an early Noisette of exquisite beauty and unknown origins, but was possibly originally 'Muscate Perpetuelle'. Deliciously fragrant

59. *Rosa indica major* is very common in old districts like Parramatta and the Hawkesbury Valley, as it was a popular 19th century rootstock rose

60. Ancient 'Tuscany' (*see* page 23) dates to *c.* 1596, an opulent rose also known as 'Old Velvet Rose'

61. Roses tumble down terraces in the Author's garden

62. The exquisite 'Little White Pet' ('Belle de Teheran') (*see* page 46) from 1879 grows to only 1 m and is perfect for the small garden. The flowers make charming posies

63. Charming 'Vick's Caprice' (1897) (*see* page 35) is one of the most moderate-growing Hybrid Perpetuals, and with its gentle sweet fragrance is ideal for small gardens

64. Old roses greet visitors at the entrance of the Author's garden

65. 'Mutabilis' (Tipo Idéale), a China rose dating back to prior to 1896 resembles nothing so much as a cloud of multi-coloured butterflies

66. 'Cornelia' (1925) (*see* page 40) is almost never out of flower and, as is characteristic of the Hybrid Musks, is very fragrant

67. A cascade of 'Leverkusen', 'Claret Cup' (*see* page 47) and 'Charles de Mills'

68. 'Chaucer' (*see* page 24), one of the exquisite English roses bred by David Austin. It has the same delicious myrrh fragrance of 'Constance Spry'

69. The Jacobite rose (*R. alba maxima*), an ancient and noble shrub rose and the emblem of Bonnie Prince Charlie

70. 'Charles Austin', a superb subtly coloured richly fragrant David Austin rose

71. Striped and cupped, sweetly fragrant and repeat flowering, 'Honorine de Brabant' (1874) (*see* page 34) is redolent of the past

72. 'Goldfinch' (1907), a small rambler with exquisite little cupped primrose to cream blooms of sweet fragrance

73. 'La Rubanée' (*see* page 33) is a popular striped Provence rose of 1845

74. 'Shropshire Lass', a breath-takingly lovely rose bred by David Austin

75. Gaily striped 'George Vibert', a Gallica of 1853

76. Old 'Fortuneana', a favourite old rambler in 19th century Australia

77. 'Perle d'Or' (1884), one of the famous Sweetheart roses, is also known as 'Yellow Cecile Brunner'

78. 'Hugo Roller' (*see* page 37), a Tea rose found in many old gardens in the Parramatta and Hawkesbury Districts

79. Pretty little 'Spong' (*see* page 46) is one of the Centifolia Pony roses of Victorian times

80. 'Mme Hardy' (*see* page 25), a Damask of 1832, is considered by many the greatest white rose ever bred

81. Exquisite and strange, loved or spurned, 'The Green Rose of China' or 'Viridiflora' (1883) (*see* page 46)

82. Lovely 'Fritz Nobis' has the blood of the eglantine rose flowing through it

83. 'York and Lancaster' (*see* page 26), an ancient Damask first recorded in 1551 has associations with the Wars of the Roses

84. 'Baronne Henriette de Snoy' (*see* page 37) (1897), a luscious creation of creamy pink, is child to 'Gloire de Dijon' (*see* page 67)

85. One of the very hardy little Spinosissima Hybrids, 'Single Cherry' (*see* page 14)

86. The 'Austrian Briar' (*see* page 16) with its dazzling display of bright golden-yellow single flowers dates back to at least the 16th century

87. A charming Hubrid Musk climber of excellent health and vigour, 'Francis E. Lester' (*see* page 21)

88. 'Rose à Parfum de l'Hay' (*see* page 43), a beautifully fragrant old Rugosa from 1901

89. Exquisite, clove fragrant *Rosa rugosa* 'Alba' (*see* page 42)

90. 'La Reine Victoria' (*see* page 31), a Bourbon from 1872, was also called 'The Shell Rose'

91. 'Fortune's Double Yellow' (*see* page 69) was introduced from China in 1842

92. 'Cramoisi Supérieur' (1832) (*see* page 46) was a popular 19th century China rose

93. 'Le Vésuve' (1825) is a China rose of complex origins and is particularly elegant and charming

94. 'Vanity' (*see* page 41), a glowing rich pink Hybrid Musk rose has the breath of sweet-peas in its heart

Old Climbing and Rambling Roses

The romance of the old rambler roses and their more adventurous climbing kin has not been lost on those who collect old roses for a hobby. The dream of roses around one's windows, rambling under the eaves, spilling over walls, creating fragrant bowers and cascading down hillsides is ever with us.

All lovers of roses must fervently (if with twentieth century discretion) echo the feelings of that great rosaria.. Dean Hole who more than once publicly expressed the desire to be bedecked, be-trellised, be-bowered, be-smothered and be-good-ness-only-knows-what-else in roses. Not to put too fine a point on it, Dean Hole liked roses.

Of all the romantic climbing roses, the Noisettes and Tea-Noisettes are surely most closely allied to our dreams. They are the epitome of what most of us think of as an old-fashioned rose: great burdens of large, double, quartered blooms of glorious rich fragrance and all the subtle colourings of the tea roses, repeat blooming, vigorous and carefree. They are the very stuff of moonlight and roses.

Once upon a time in that ultimate of all moon-light and roses cities, Charleston in South Carolina, there was a rice growing farmer called John Champney. Mr Champney grew in his garden the late summer-flowering, true and very fragrant Musk rose, one of the few good climbing roses then available. In the same garden was that good and gay China rose 'Old Blush' (also known at that time as 'Parson's Pink China'). By whatever means (and the story differs according to the teller at this point), a seedling climber originated from John Champ-ney's garden in 1802, a rose which combined the virtues of both parents. It bore fragrant pink flowers in clusters and was summer flowering. The rose found favour, both in the United States and Europe, and became known as 'Champney's Pink Cluster'.

A French nurseryman living in Charleston,

Phillipe Noisette, sowed seed of 'Champney's Pink Cluster'. The resulting seedlings demonstrated one of the classic rose inheritance patterns: the offspring of the union of a once flowering rose with a remon-tant (repeat flowering) rose are all once flowering, but the grandchildren of such a mating create a remontant line.

In the resulting batch of seedlings raised by Phillipe Noisette was a lax shrub to 3 m which had clusters of small, cupped, semi-double blooms, initially a deep old rose in colour, fading to a soft pale creamy-pink, with a rich clove fragrance. It had tremendous freedom of bloom and the combina-tion of extreme floriferousness, dependable repeat flowerings and fragrance ensured that it would become extensively planted and retained in gardens throughout the USA and Europe.

Phillipe had a brother in Paris, a nurseryman called Louis Noisette, to whom this rose was sent around 1814. It was painted by Redouté in 1821 in the gardens of Malmaison. The rose named 'Blush' by Phillipe Noisette was named by Louis 'Le Rosier de Phillipe Noisette'. Redoutés's painting was titled *R. noisettiana*. Along the way this charming climber became variously known as 'Blush Noisette', 'Old Blush Noisette', 'French Noisette' and *R.* × *noisettiana*. To this might be added local names and names from other non-English speaking countries. For instance, Mrs Gore called it 'Flesh-coloured Noisette', and at least one English nursery sold it as 'Blush Cluster'.

One suspects that more than one seedling rose was raised by Phillipe Noisette, because Ethelyn Emery Keays described a rose in Calvert County, Maryland, which could be dated back to the Civil War. Called locally 'Faded Pink Monthly', this sweetly named rose was described as being very lovely, of less than half the stature of 'Blush Noisette' but in all other respects a rose that might have sat for Redouté's portrait of its more famous relative. It could of course have been a dwarf sport from 'Blush Noisette', but it is only too likely that Phillipe raised a batch of seedlings rather than one.

'Autumnalis' (plate 58) remains one of my favourite Noisettes and is surprisingly rare on world listings. Clusters of pink-tinted creamy little buds in downward hanging posies open to semi-double, silky little blooms of a creamy-milk shade showing clusters of golden stamens and cupping a delicious fragrance. The almost thornless branches are 'zig-zagged', and it clearly has *Rosa moschata* in its heritage. G.S. Thomas, who delights in this lovely rose and spent much time researching it, says that it has mysterious origins, having been first mentioned, as well as he can detect, in a Daisy Hill Nursery catalogue of 1912. No prior literature includes the name 'Autumnalis' and he is of the opinion that it may be a renamed Noisette of very early origin such as 'Muscata Perpetuelle'. It certainly has the look of the early Noisette and is quite uncharacteristic of the roses bred around 1912.

Around the oldest colonial properties in Australia and in the oldest areas of cemeteries such as Gore Hill and Rookwood may be seen a number of plants of *R.* × *noisettiana manettii* usually known as 'Manettii'. It is a semi-climbing shrub rose of real charm with sweetly fragrant pink blooms which show the China influence. It was used as a rootstock in the nineteenth century and has the reputation of enabling roses budded on to it to flower earlier. I shudder at the number of rootstock roses rambling over the old graveyards. Charming though I find them, each represents a lost rose. How many Hybrid Perpetuals and Teas, for instance, were lost forever through the overwhelming suckering strength of the rootstock? But perhaps the endless droughts and fires of this country should be asked to take their share of the blame. Regeneration by suckering is impossible for the budded rose, as it has no direct contact with the ground.

Amongst the oldest remaining Noisette roses is the delightful 'Aimée Vibert', a remontant climber said to be a hybrid between 'Champney's Pink Cluster' and *R. sempervirens*. It was also known as 'Bouquet de la Mariée' and 'Nivea'. The clusters of fragrant double white flowers open from pink-tinted buds and are set off by the glossy dark leaves of its *R. sempervirens* parent. A number of tantalising early Noisettes are described by Ethelyn Emery Keays in *Old Roses*, all of which were received by her from various old colonial properties in Maryland.

It was not long before the blood of the early Noisettes was mingled with that of 'Parks' Yellow Tea-scented China' and the result was the Tea-Noisettes, as glorious a group of roses as any the world has yet seen.

'Lamarque' (plate 36) is an historic rose of 1830 which resulted from a cross between 'Blush Noisette' and 'Parks' Yellow Tea-scented China', and was raised by a shoe-maker in Angers according to the famous rosarian, the Rev. Joseph Pemberton. It was released by M. Maréchal of Angers in 1830, and was originally known as 'Thé Maréchal'. Few roses evoke warm moonlit summer nights as does 'Lamarque'. She smothers in great burdens of nodding blossoms, very double, flat, with quilled and quartered petals that begin a fresh lemon-white changing to pure white. The scent is exquisite, a pure fine tea fragrance; the foliage smooth, shining and dark green. 'Lamarque' is relatively remontant, reflowering well in Autumn.

Some roses inspire such affection and admiration that they acquire compliments wherever they go. Canon Ellacombe (how gentlemen of the cloth do recur through the story of the rose!) wrote a delightful book *In a Gloucestershire Garden* in 1895. This book was most deservedly recently republished by Century Publishing Company, London. Of 'Lamarque' he said: 'The old rose 'Lamarque' deserves a grateful record. It has always been a great favourite with me, and when in its full beauty I think it almost the most beautiful of white roses … If I were limited to only one white rose I think I should choose Lamarque.' Mrs Earle, in her equally famous book *Pot Pourri from a Surrey Garden*, now alas only to be found occasionally, in second-hand book shops, said that no garden was perfect without a 'Lamarque' rose in it. And from another writer: 'The flowers are of purest white—the dense white of the waterlily, and their great moon-pale cups lie wide, like marble blossoms carved in low relief, exhaling an exquisite odour'.

As you swoon beneath the fragrant weight of Lamarquian prose, let us add from *The Floral World*, published in 1874, the following: 'The mammoth rose-tree of Santa Rosa is, we think, of sufficient importance to justify its being noticed in these pages. This immense rose-tree now clothing the cottage of a Mr Rendall, of Santa Rosa, is an example of our old friend Lamarque, one of the finest of Noisette roses. It covers an area of four hundred superficial feet, and in due season is fairly loaded with flowers. Indeed, so profusely does it bloom, that it has had no less than four thousand fully expanded roses and twenty thousand buds at one time. It appears to have been planted fifteen years since, and so vigorous has been the growth from the first, that it now extends over the roof of the house, and when in bloom presents a magnificent sight.'

Let me simply add that 'Lamarque' was the progenitor of that other delicious fragrant glory of the Victorian era, the Tea roses.

From the same magic year comes another exquisite Tea-Noisette, 'Deprez à Fleur Jaune', of the same parentage as 'Lamarque'. It needs the gentler climate of Australia, the southern United States and the Mediterranean region to show this superb Noisette at her best and most vigorous. The flowers borne singly and in small clusters open from pink and apricot buds to reveal large, very double, flat silky-textured blooms that are creamy lemon, often flushed with apricot-pink, peach and yellow. The autumnal blooms are often the most exquisite of all. They have a powerful and delicious fruity tea fragrance that equals the beauty of the flower. It has few prickles, is well clothed with light green foliage and one could not wish for anything more beautiful than this rose in full flower. Jack Harkness describes the flowers as giving 'the impression of soaking up the sun's warmth and paying it back in a sleepy scent'. In his *Manual of Roses* (1846), Prince wrote, 'It is so powerfully fragrant that one plant will perfume a large garden in the cool weather of autumn'. This rose was sold as 'Jaune Deprez' and 'Noisette Deprez'.

Dean Hole named 'Gloire de Dijon' (plate 84) as his favourite rose. 'Were I condemned to have but one rose for the rest of my life, I should ask, before leaving the dock, to be presented with a strong plant of 'Gloire de Dijon'.' It would surprise no one who knew both roses that 'Gloire de Dijon' had 'Souvenir de la Malmaison' for one parent. The other, according to oral tradition, was a vigorous unnamed climbing yellow Tea rose. 'Gloire de Dijon' is very remontant, and has blooms of similar form to 'Deprez à Fleur Jaune', but the whole effect is warmer, being buff-yellow, suffused with peach pink and apricot of various depths according to the day, but always exquisite. The rich fragrance is delicious. It often went under the name of 'Old Glory' in England.

'Cloth of Gold' (plate 13)—'round and deep, each flower presents such a chalice of pure gold as Hebe might have presented to the Gods'—is one of the most stunning of all climbing roses. It is not for the very cold climates of northern England and Europe, but in the Mediterranean countries, in the southern USA, and in Australia, 'Cloth of Gold' is a rose of dreams. It is said to be a self-set seedling of 'Lamarque' and was released by Coquereau in 1843, becoming available here by 1860. It caused a sensation when it was exhibited at the Third National Rose Show in England at the Crystal Palace. The nodding tulip-shaped roses are of pure soft gold, the whole plant very floriferous and remontant. The fragrance is a delicious fruity tea mixture. This rose is also known as 'Chromatella'.

'Celine Forestier' (plate 48) was released by Trouillard in 1842 and is one of the most exquisite of all the old Tea Noisettes. Tight buds borne singly or in small clusters open to exquisite double, creamy pale gold, quartered blooms with button eye and and intense and delicious spicy Tea fragrance. It is very remontant once established, which it does surely but slowly, to eventually become a vigorous and tough climber. It is said to have arisen from a cross between 'Lamarque' and 'Deprez à Fleur Jaune'.

'Claire Jacquier', yet another of these glorious golden French beauties, originated from A. Bernaix near Lyon in 1888. It has large, silky, double flat, quartered blooms with a button eye in yolk yellow. It has a delicious fragrance with more than a dash of Tea about it, and the flowers come endlessly in small sprays in spring, later in huge multiheaded sprays.

'Alister Stella Gray' is a rose that has evoked many delightful memories. It was raised by a famous amateur rose breeder, particularly of Tea roses, Mr Alexander Hill Gray of Bath. It was introduced commercially in 1894 and was sold in the United States as 'Golden Rambler'. This rose produces clusters of exquisite tight apricot-yellow buds which open to double flat blooms, quartered with a button eye, often paling in colour around the edges. The fragrance is deliciously sweet with a dash of Tea rose in it. This rose is to be found on old graves at Rookwood cemetery and in old gardens. It is a slow starter but vigorous once established and long lived.

Another old Rookwood rose is 'Crépuscule' (plate 15) (1904), which is also to be found occasionally in old and abandoned gardens in NSW. The loosely formed semi-double blooms are a lovely shade of old gold and the whole shrub-climber (to 3 m) covers in fragrant blooms. The patterns of rose usage differ greatly in Australia whether one looks at colonial plantings or modern. 'Crépuscule' was recently imported into South Australia for propagation and distribution as it was uncommon there, only for it to be detected at Rookwood and elsewhere in NSW.

'Madame Alfred Carrière' (plate 7) is among my favourite roses. What a fragrance she has, all sweetness and refinement. We have planted her where everyone may pass by and sniff deeply into her creamy cupped double blooms with their faint delicate blush. She is very remontant and very floriferous and was released by J. Schwartz of Lyon in 1879. The foliage is soft and of a delicate light green.

The primrose way of Tea-Noisettes, as Ethelyn Emery Keays called it, led to three more luscious climbers in the golden colour range. 'Maréchal Niel' was a sensation when it was released in 1864 by Pradel. It was said to be a seedling of 'Cloth of Gold', which is entirely possible when the two blooms are placed side by side. It is the softest, purest, butteriest yellow in colour, a nodding elegant bloom of unsurpassed rich scent. It was much too tender with its Tea blood for the cold shores of England, but in warmer drier climes it is one of the most superlatively beautiful roses ever bred. Few roses can do so much for a pergola or trellis, smothering as it does with chalice-like blooms of a luscious rich fragrance best described as a mixture of fresh wild strawberries and Tea roses. It is a rose, as this writer has amply illustrated, which drives rose lovers to superlatives. To show that I am not alone, here are a few quotations from others who have fallen beneath its spell. Graham Stuart Thomas said of it, 'Nothing so yellow, so voluptuous, so fragrant of Tea has been seen before'. The great rosarian Foster-Milliar called it 'Quite unapproachable', while Alfred Prince said it could be named with the eyes closed by its scent alone. Ethelyn Emery Keays described it as 'very large and deep, full to the brim, very highly scented ... a rose to be looked up to from below'. 'Maréchal Niel' was only successful under glass in England other than in the south-western counties. How fortunate we are in this warmer climate to be able to grow it to the perfection and peaceful old age it surely deserves.

'William Allen Richardson' evokes strong affections among those who know it. It is one of the most asked for roses among older rose lovers, who speak of its glories with wistfulness. Jack Harkness reports

exactly the same symptoms among English rose growers. This rose, released by the widow Ducher in 1878, was said to be a sport of 'Rêve d'Or' ('Golden Chain' in the USA), which had also been released by the widow Ducher in 1869. It was a very successful and popular climber with buff yellow blooms. The seed parent of 'Rêve d'Or' was said to be a Tea rose, 'Mme Schultz', which was in turn a descendent of the great 'Lamarque', 'William Allen Richardson' resembles 'Rêve d'Or' in all ways other than colour, which is a rich deep orange-gold paling toward the edges of neat, quartered blooms with Tea fragrance. Both roses are very remontant.

Climbing Tea roses have a charm all their own, with luscious elegant blooms filled with sleepy summery Tea scents, their delicate purity of colouring and their bounteousness of bloom from early summer to late autumn, even to the virtual end of winter in most parts of Australia. They rest a mere two or three weeks in late July to early August with us, before releafing and covering in buds. Some are climbing mutations of bush Tea roses, others are climbers in their own right. As Graham Stuart Thomas said, 'They are too good to lose forever; the gentle elegance of bygone days is preserved in them'.

'Sombrieul' 1851 is perhaps the greatest of all the climbing Tea rose treasures, which is to say it is a rose of surpassing perfection. It is like a refined 'Souvenir de la Malmaison', flat, very double, quartered, and of great beauty, creamy white with just the hint of a flesh tint in the centre. It has the most delicious, rich summery depths of fragrance to be inhaled over and over. 'Sombrieul' is a rose to be treasured for all time. The blooms come singly and in small clusters and the foliage is thick dark green and leathery. In its blood flows Bourbon, Tea rose and Hybrid Perpetual ancestry, which explains its resemblance to the great 'Souvenir de la Malmaison'.

'Reine Marie Henriette' is one of the great nostalgia roses of all time. It was released by Levet in 1878 and was said to be the result of a cross between 'Mme Berard', a very old pale yellow Tea with blooms streaked red on the outside and flushed rose inside, and 'General Jacqueminot', the superb old deep red Hybrid Perpetual. In its bloodline therefore it includes 'Madame Falcot' (1858), a Tea rose in the style and colour of 'Safrano' and 'Gloire de Dijon'. The result, despite the complexities of its breeding, is decidedly Tea-like with large cupped double blooms which have large guard petals and lesser inner petals of a pure glowing cherry crimson, fragrant and free-blooming. It is one of those roses which proclaims the joy in its heart. In modern days, another totally dissimilar rose has struck me with its joyous assertion of life, 'Freude'. It obviously appealed to its breeder, Kordes, in just the same way, for its name when translated into English means 'joy'. Ethelyn Emery Keays similarly responded to 'Reine Marie Henriette', for she spoke of it as 'glowing with life and most desirable to look upon—a vigorous, free blooming happy rose'.

The climbing form of 'Mrs Herbert Stevens' is a rose of true refinement, as befits the daughter of 'Niphetos' and 'Frau Karl Druschki'. The good Frau confers greater substance to the pure white petals than is possessed by the airily delicate paper-like petals of 'Niphetos', but the elegance of the great old Tea rose is retained. By breeding it must be a Hybrid Tea, but by every other character it is unmistakeably a Tea rose. The colour is creamy white with a hint of lemon, the buds long and elegant, the fragrance rich and superb with more than a little of the freesia in its composition.

The climbing form of 'Lady Hillingdon' was released in 1917, and arose by sporting from the magnificent shrub rose of 1910. The colour and fragrance have no match elsewhere in the rose world. The elegant long buds open to gracious semi-double tulip-shaped nodding blooms of softest richest apricot yellow, offset by beautiful plum-coloured foliage. In the cool hours of morning the fragrance is of ripe apricots, while later in the day the famous Tea scent blends and then predominates. It is a vigorous climber to 7 m or more and will bear endless blooms until early winter.

'Solfaterre' (1843) was a seedling of 'Lamarque' and favours the Tea side of its ancestry. It belongs among the climbing Tea roses in spirit, if not in strict definition. This graceful rose has sulphur yellow, very large double flowers of delicious fragrance. Like most of the 'primrose way' roses, it found its Shangrila in Australia and in other warm climes such as the Azores, the Canary Islands, the Mediterranean and southern USA, in all of which places it is a magnificent rose.

In 1898 Bernaix introduced 'Souvenir de Madame Léonie Viennot'. It is a richly coloured climbing rose with coral red buds opening to loosely double, deliciously Tea-fragrant, clear gold blooms with a heavy blush of copper-pink to copper red.

Like all its lovely kin, it is very repeat flowering, and will grow to 5–7 m in height.

'Fortune's Double Yellow' (plate 91) is a marvellously coloured rose. The base colour of the loose semi-double blooms is a delicate rich yellow heavily flushed with pure pink to create a luminous glory of colour. It is also known as R. × odorata pseudinica, 'Beauty of Glazenwood', 'San Rafael Rose', and 'Gold of Ophir', and was one of Robert Fortune's most exciting introductions from China (1845). It was a brilliantly coloured rose for its time, and as G.S. Thomas says 'will make people blink even today'. It was already known to be a very old rose when Robert Fortune 'discovered' it in a rich Mandarin's garden at Ningpo in 1842. In Robert Fortune's own words: 'On entering one of the gardens on a fine morning in May I was struck by a mass of yellow flowers which completely covered a distant part of the wall; the colour was not a common yellow, but had something of buff in it, which gave the flower a striking and uncommon appearance. I immediately ran up to the place, and to my surprise and delight found that I had discovered a most beautiful new climbing rose.' It was sent in a Wardian case back to England, where it was known to be growing by 1845.

One other climbing sport of a rose must surely be mentioned, for it is outstanding in every respect, 'Climbing Devoniensis' or the 'Magnolia Rose' which was introduced in 1858. This rose is pure clotted Devonshire cream! The blooms are large, very double, with thick velvety cream petals, opening cupped and quartered and full to the brim with rich tea fragrance. It sometimes acquires a flush of apricot in the heart after opening. The foliage of this magnificent old Tea is dark, shiny and an excellent foil to the flowers. Like all the Tea roses it blooms its heart out from spring to early winter.

Two splendid pillar roses (or short climbers) should also be mentioned, 'Mme Charles' and 'Noella Nabonnand'. The good and sweet 'Mme Charles' (1864) is one of those defenceless innocent-looking roses which seem to arouse protective instincts in the gardener, yet she is as tough as they come. From particularly lovely buds emerge open, semi-double flowers of light pink with deeper pink reverse, sweetly fragrant, borne in large heads of bloom throughout the season.

'Noella Nabonnand' (1901) is a rose that seems to wear a mantle of rich rose silk. The semi-double blooms borne in great quantity are of the richest

shade of pink with a silken sheen. The scent is deliciously Tea rose, and the whole is set off by plum-
tinted young foliage. It will grow to around 2.5 m.

Some roses are symbols of an era. 'Tea
Rambler' (plates 2 and 38) (1904) is one of them.
Born into the golden summers of the Edwardian
age, with great powder puffs of rosy-salmon blooms
with a warm rich Tea scent, it is the ideal rose to
share tea-on-the-lawn with on drowsy summer
afternoons, or to embower a gateway or verandah.

Many of the old Tea roses developed climbing
forms as the years went by, often giving new
impetus to their sales, as the search for novelty by
gardeners is no new phenomenon. Among those
still to be found commercially around the world are
the climbing forms of 'Madamoiselle Franziska
Kruger' (1880), 'Madame Falcot' (1858), 'Marie
Van Houtte' (1871), 'General Schlablikine' (1878),
'Niphetos' (1889), 'Papa Gontier' (1904),
'Souvenir d'un Ami' (1846), 'Penelope' and others.

More than one rose breeder has been unable to
resist hybridising *Rosa gigantea* which, together with
R. chinensis, are speculated to be the parents of
'Hume's Blush Tea-scented China' (*R. × odorata*)
and its variety *R. × odorata ochroleuca*, otherwise
known as 'Parks' Yellow Tea-scented China'. *Rosa
gigantea*, fortunately for its namer, did turn out to be
the largest species rose ever discovered. The flowers
are creamy white, very large and single, and are the
origin of the characteristic Tea scent of its progeny,
for it bears this fragrance in abundance. It is a
tender rose and fares badly in colder climates than
those of mainland Australia. To date its offspring
have been magnificent in Mediterranean countries,
Australia and other sympathetic climates, but
resent very severe frosts. All *R. gigantea* offspring
have characteristics which place them, not unexpectedly, securely with the Tea roses.

'Belle Portugaise' was introduced in 1903 and
was raised by Henri Cayeux of the Lisbon Botanical
Garden. One of the parents is agreed upon as *R.
gigantea*, but the other parent is in dispute, although
generally quoted as 'Reine Marie Henriette'. The
loosely double flowers open from long elegant buds
and are composed of large silky petals, light creamy
salmon pink on the inside, deeper pink on the
outside and rolled at the edges. Its Tea scent is
delicious and it is a gracious summery rose. It will
grow comfortably to 7 m. Its companion, 'La
Follette', was raised at Cannes by Lord Brough-
ham's gardener, Brisby, around 1910. It is much

like 'Belle Portugaise' in form but is much richer in
colouring, the inner petals being a luscious suffusion of cream and rose, the reverse a coppery
salmon-pink deepening to crimson. It is vigorous
and will easily climb 7 m or more and as wide. A
fitting companion in spirit, if not by breeding, is
'Madame Grégoire Staechlin' (plate 27) which was
released in 1927 by Dot. Its other name is 'Spanish
Beauty'. The large open generous semi-double
blooms are composed of large petals of a glowing
pink with deeper pink reverse and smother the rose
for one glorious airy display in springtime. Breathe
in the delicious fragrance of old-fashioned sweet-
peas and you will fall in love forever with this glory
of warmer climes. There is no point in dead-
heading a once-flowering climber so let this glowing
lady develop her huge pear-shaped golden heps.
The wonderful *Roses of Yesterday and Today*
catalogues put out by Lester and Tillotson in the
USA used to contain the following delightful
comment on 'Mme Grégoire Staechlin': 'Its fairy-
airy loveliness reminds one of that sweet young
thing who passes you at garden parties looking cool,
fresh, and altogether charming, in organdie and
garden hat'. How true!

In Australia, Alister Clark of Bulla, Victoria also
succumbed to the charms of a large *R. gigantea*
growing in his garden and carried out many crosses
with it. 'Lorraine Lee' has the look of a Tea rose
about it. The elegant buds open to medium sized
semi-double blooms in a rich rosey apricot pink
with an apricot glow in the heart. The fragrance is
stunning, a delicious mixture of fruitiness and tea
fragrance. Its parentage was said to be 'Jessie
Clark' (a seedling of *R. gigantea*) × 'Capitaine
Miller' (a seedling of 'General Schlablikine', a
China rose). It was released in 1924 by Hackett and
Company of Adelaide. It is a superb hedging plant
with the additional blessing of flowering very well
during the winter months. The climbing form is
superb. An old one on our own property smothers
in blooms in several flushes throughout the year and
the fragrance is wonderful. While it is one of the
best of all climbers in a warmer climate, it
apparently grows vigorously but flowers little in
England. Jack Harkness said that the one grown at
Hitchin by his family elicited the gibe 'that one
needed binoculars to study the few flowers it bore'.

'Harbinger' (1923), another of Alister Clark's
crosses with the giant-flowered Burmese species *R.
gigantea*, has extraordinary glowing large floppy
fragrant single flowers in a blend of pinks. It has

one magnificent crop of blooms, both heavy and spectacular. The trick with all these Clark climbers is to prune, if prune you must, in late summer for late winter and early spring blooming. Clark released a whole line of roses raised from the Giant Rose of Burma and they have become collectors' items. Each one retrieved from extinction is a contribution both to Australia's and the world's heritage of unusual and beautiful roses.

Some *R. gigantea* derived climbing roses bred by Alister Clark that are well worth seeking out and are still known in cultivation are: 'Doris Downs' (1932) with large very fragrant, semi-double cupped blooms of pink to light red; 'Kitty Kininmonth' (1922) has deep glowing pink cupped semi-double blooms; 'Jessie Clark' (1915) clothed in large airy single bright rose pink blooms; 'Nancy Hayward' (1937), a huge glowing single tomato red; and 'Flying Colours' (1922), a rambler with light red single blooms in great abundance.

Canon Ellacombe in his much loved *In a Gloucestershire Garden* wrote, 'The *Rosa multiflora*, a charming rose, rightly so named, for though the flowers are individually small, the trusses of flowers are wonderful; I have counted on one truss (meaning by that the part projecting from the leaves) over six hundred flowers. This species also is the parent of many hybrids, but in all of them one curious resemblance to the parent is always seen in finely serrated stipules; each stipule is like the finest saw.' It is native to Japan and Korea and was first recorded in 1696. Its powerful and delicious fruity fragrance is freely borne through the air, and its enormous trusses of tiny single white blooms, fragrance and climbing habits were all gifts to the hybridist. It was an ancestor of the Polyantha line of roses, which in turn evolved into today's Floribundas. Only one climbing form of the species, a romantically named one at that, is still grown widely today. Its name is the 'Seven Sisters Rose' or *R. multiflora platyphylla*. It was cultivated in China and found its way to England in 1815. It bears huge trusses of small flowers which vary from light pink through to deep lilac pink, hence the name.

A number of hybrid *R. multiflora* climbers are still grown with great affection today. 'Goldfinch' (plate 72) is one of my own favourites. The little yellow blooms in clusters are borne with abandon in a single prolonged flowering on a healthy, all but thornless, medium climber. The buds begin yolk yellow but gently fade to lemon and cream in hot sunshine, not at all displeasingly, and the blooms emit an intense fragrance of oranges and bananas.

'Tausendschön' or the 'Thousand Beauties Rose', which has in its ancentry *R. multiflora*, the first Polyantha 'Paquerette' and the great Hybrid Perpetual 'General Jacqueminot', was introduced in 1906. It is a graceful light-stemmed, almost thornless rose and the long branches are laden with clusters of small flowers in many shades of pink. It is a gay rose and a lovely sight.

'Paul's Scarlet Climber' was introduced into gardens in 1916. It is a hardy and long-lived climber, not very large, and the semi-double flowers borne in profusion are a vivid scarlet, fading to crimson. It is once flowering. A form called 'Blaze' was released in the United States in 1932 which was supposedly remontant, but has proved not to be reliably so.

'Aglaia' (1896), the first yellow-flowered rambler bred, resulted from a cross between *R. multiflora* and that brave new world rose 'Rêve d'Or'. It has lovely semi-double, cupped, pale yellow intensely fragrant blooms which fade gently and gracefully to creamy lemon. It was to play an important role in creating the Musk Hybrids.

'The Garland' is a hybrid between *R. multiflora* (probably *R. multiflora carnea*) and *R. moschata*, and was raised by a Mr Wells of Tunbridge Wells, Kent. It was introduced in 1835 and bears immense quantities of creamy salmon buds opening to faintly blushed cream and milky white blooms with rich orange fragrance that carries on the air. Looking rather like 'The Garland' is the marvellously named 'Rambling Rector' (1912) with creamy semi-double flowers in clusters, quite overpowering for the superb abundance of its blooms and its delicious fruity fragrance. Both will form large cascading shrubs if this is preferred to using them as climbers.

The first red climbing rose ever to be introduced into Europe was 'Crimson Rambler'. In Chinese gardens it was known as *shi-tz-mei* or 'Ten Sister', while to Japanese gardeners it was known as *soukara ibara*. In Edinburgh, where it was originally sent by its discoverer, an engineer called Robert Smith, it was called 'Engineer's Rose'. It was officially introduced into the rose trade in 1893 as 'Turner's Crimson Rambler' by Charles Turner, a nurseryman of Slough. It was a landmark rose in the development of ramblers. From it were bred three charming ramblers, 'Blush Rambler' (1903) which resulted from a cross with 'The Garland', and 'Veilchenblau' (1909), a seedling of the 'Crimson Rambler' and 'Hiawatha' (1904).

Some roses are so bright and cheeky that they must evoke affection. Such a one is 'Hiawatha' (1904), which resulted from a cross between 'Crimson Rambler' and 'Paul's Carmine Pillar'. It bears masses of quite large single flowers in large heads, of a bright cherry red with a creamy white centre. If you have a soft spot for the occasional cheery cheeky fellow in your garden, then plant 'Hiawatha' on a trellis or archway.

'Blush Rambler' is a refined rose, almost thornless, with deliciously fragrant cupped semi-double flowers of light pink borne in clusters. 'Veilchenblau' ('Violet Blue' literally) is a lovely thornless rambling rose with masses of soft light lilac blooms which give any garden an instant grandmotherly look, especially if combined with lots of lavenders. Each little flower has a tiny white eye and the petals are frequently streaked with fine white. To all this desirability, 'Veilchenblau' adds the sweet fragrance of fresh green apples.

Fitting companions for 'Veilchenblau' are the almost thornless 'Rose Marie Viaud' (1924), with very double flowers like little rosettes borne in large bunches and of a gorgeous shade of parma violet, and 'Violette' (1921), apple-scented with large trusses of blooms that ring a subtle and sophisticated colour change from intense crimson-purple to maroon and purple, and finally crimson-grey as the blooms age.

If 'Turner's Crimson Rambler' was to cause a sensation in its day (it had enormous sales and even Queen Victoria was said to have journeyed to Slough to see it!), it was left to the Wichuriana ramblers (and trailers) to drive gardeners crazy with desire for red climbing roses and to become the epitome of the late Victorian and Edwardian bower roses. Not that red roses were the only colour produced. Far from it. The Wichurianas were strong on creams, whites, pinks and reds, but yellows and even amber roses were bred. They usually inherit the beautifully polished leaves of the parent, and more often than not the fragrance of apples. In some the fragrance is of rich ripe apples, in others of green apples.

The most famous of all the Wichurianas must certainly be 'Dorothy Perkins' (1901). It flowers its heart out for nearly a month, covering in clusters of bright double pink little blooms. It is utterly essential to the Edwardian garden, draped around a porch or over an archway. Somewhat surprisingly its other parent was an old pink Hybrid Perpetual 'Madame Gabriel Luizet'. 'Debutante' (1902) is much like the gay Dorothy and results from a similar cross involving, in this instance, the superb pink Hybrid Perpetual 'Baroness Rothschild'. This is an altogether charming rose, with cupped and quilled blooms of clear rose pink paling to blush, borne in dainty sprays and with a delicate cowslip fragrance.

'Alberic Barbier' (1900) is an almost indecently vigorous healthy climber, resulting from the marriage of R. wichuriana and a Tea rose, 'Shirley Hibberd'—and what an off-spring they had! The blooms begin as beautifully formed soft lemon yellow buds opening to creamy white medium-sized double flowers with the clean rich fragrance of fresh green apples. All this is accompanied by clean glossy deep green foliage that laughs at disease; it smothers in roses when flowering, and it is repeat flowering in the autumn. A worthy companion is 'Aviateur Bleriot', a Wichuriana of 1910 vintage with delightful small blooms of perfect form in a soft warm yellow that smother a climber with dense, dark, glossy foliage.

A climber almost too lovely for comparison is 'Albertine' (plate 22) (1921), which resulted when R. wichuriana was crossed with a lovely coppery old Hybrid Tea 'Mrs A.R. Waddell'. It creates an unforgettable late spring to early summer display, bearing huge quantities of salmon-red buds which open to large semi-double coppery pink blooms which change in time to light pink. The rich fragrance is unforgettable. It will easily reach 6–7 m on a wall and is outstandingly vigorous. In the larger garden it will create a breathtaking sight if allowed to mount up into a large shrub or permitted to throw the occasional careless embrace around a tall shrub or a tree.

One of the most popular Wichuriana ramblers is 'François Juranville', bred by the prolific and successful rose breeder Barbier in 1906. It resulted from a cross with the estimable China rose 'Mme Laurette Messimy'. It has great vigour and charm, smothering with huge quilled and quartered flat double blooms which are a bright salmon pink, suffused at the base with an apricot glow. The fragrance, as one comes to expect of the group, is of fresh sweet apples. It is a delight on pergolas, arches and around a verandah.

'Emily Gray' is considered the best of all the

yellow Wichurianas, not the strong brilliant yellow of today but a soft warm buff yellow far easier to place in the garden. Opening from pretty little buds, the flowers are semi-double and beautifully fragrant.

The Wichurianas were hybridised with the greatest enthusiasm in their heyday, and it would be perfectly possible to write a book devoted to them. However, I will only briefly recommend the following, all worthy to take their place beside the ones described above: 'Dr. Huey' (1920), a cupped semi-double bright crimson with more than a hint of China about it, which is not surprising as both Tea and China run in its bloodline; 'Augustine Gervais' (1918), a large flowered bicolour with creamy-apricot inside petals and coppery-pink reverse, deliciously fragrant; 'Gerbe Rose' (1904), a very remontant, almost thornless pillar rose with large cupped loosely double creamy pink, quartered blooms with the fragrance, as G.S. Thomas so accurately describes it, resembling white paeonies; 'Gardenia' (1899) resulted from a cross with that great yellow Tea rose 'Perle des Jardins', and the apple-scented prolific blooms are very double, cupped and quartered, of creamy white with a warm yellow centre fading to nearly white; 'Dr W. van Fleet' (1910) and its remontant but otherwise similar sport 'New Dawn' (plate 40), with large, semi-double, floppy, fragrant blush pink blooms; and lastly, in a very incomplete list of those that are still to be found by the old rose collector, 'La Perle' (1904), not unlike 'Alberic Barbier', but with a hint of green in the creamy white and an intense and delicious fragrance compounded of lemons, tea scent, and green apples. And on that exceeding fragrant memory of the past, we leave the Wichurianas for a smaller group of climbers of equally stunning beauty, abundance, fragrance and suitability to the older garden.

It was the French rose breeders who experimented with *R. sempervirens*, as indeed they did with so many of our inheritance of great climbing roses of the past. And of all the French hybridists, M. Jacques was by far the most successful. The temptation to use this species lay in the evergreen nature of the shiny green leaves, but only two of these roses are still to be bought from specialist nurseries in the world, 'Adélaïde d'Orléans' and 'Félicité et Perpétué'.

'Adélaïde d'Orléans' (1826), named for the youngest daughter of the then Duc d'Orléans and raised by his gardener M. Jacques at the Chateau of Neuilly, can best be likened to a weeping double Japanese cherry blossom tree. It is once-flowering, but of such exquisite loveliness that it is well worth a year of waiting. The blooms hang in clusters, the buds a deep rose pink opening to creamy pink graduating to blush white in the centre, with pale yellow stamens and delicate primrose fragrance.

'Félicité et Perpétué' (1827) was named for M. Jacques' daughters who were called after St Felicitas and St Perpetua. Their Saint's Day is 7 May. These martyrs were thrown to wild beasts in Carthage in AD 203. Many a gardener not too well versed in religious history has planted this rose in the fond belief that it is ever-blooming but, alas, like its sister rose 'Adélaide d'Orléans' it is too beautiful to be accorded more than once a year to mere mortals. Against a background of shining dark green leaves, in due season 'Félicité et Perpétué' covers herself in a breathtaking veil of milk-white perfect double flowers with tiny button eyes which open from crimson blushed buds. With her sister she shares that most ephemeral and delicate of woodland fragrances, that of primroses. Despite their exquisite beauty, both of these roses are hardy in even the coldest of climates.

Two other *sempervirens* ramblers are still available in England: 'Flora' with masses of large globular deep pink blooms, and 'Princess Louise' with clusters of crimson-tinted buds opening to creamy-white double blooms of a delicious and penetrating fruity fragrance.

It is easy to forget that Hybrid Tea roses date back to the 1850s, so that some old climbing Hybrid Teas are rightly mentioned among old-fashioned roses. As well, from time to time, there arise roses that are clearly in the old style or even that of wild roses. That they survive the extreme pressures of selection in seedling trials for Hybrid Tea form says much for their charm and appeal. When they persist for several decades in commercial lists they are clearly remarkable. As well there are a scattered group of climbers which are best considered here. They come principally from the Boursaults, the Bourbons and the Hybrid Perpetuals.

The Boursaults were a kind of evolutionary dead-end for rose breeders. Beautiful though they were, they were sterile. As a first generation cross between the remontant China rose and the non-remontant *R. pendulina*, the Boursaults were non-remotant as that is the dominant trait. A rose breeder can normally throw remontant roses in the second generation, but as the Boursaults were sterile . . . no second generation.

The only Boursault to still be listed by most specialist nurseries is 'Mme Sancy de Parabere'. In America it became known as 'Virginian Lass'. It is a charming rose, large-flowered and generally considered the most beautiful of the boursaults. The individual blooms are double, fully 12–12.5 cm across, forming a saucer-like bloom with the outer petals much larger than the inner petals. They nod elegantly and are sweetly scented. While only once flowering, it is very floriferous and has the added benefit of being completely thornless. A smaller-flowered Boursault, 'Amadis', is still available commercially from a very few specialist nurseries around the world and is to be seen at Sissinghurst.

'Zepherine Drouhin' is another thornless rose, a Bourbon upon which the plot of one of Agatha Christie's novels hinged. Its alternative name is the 'Thornless Rose', although in fact it does have just the occasional prickle, alas for Miss Christie's plot. It makes an excellent pillar rose or for use over arbours and arches. The cerise pink is, one warns, bright, so it should never be placed against an unsympathetically coloured background. I like Jack Harkness above all other writers about roses and cannot help but quote his comments on 'Zepherine Drouhin': 'But let them open and the small flowers express the warmth of the summer, not this summer but some old remembered days of warmth, when roses innocently quartered their centres without disgrace, and were expected to breathe a gentle fragrance into the air'. If you would care for a lovely pale pink version, a sport called 'Kathleen Harrop' exists, in all respects other than colour, the same.

'Blairii No.2' (1845) was, regrettably, the only name Mr Blair managed to coax out of the air for this lovely rose. It is best grown as a pillar rose and bears masses of very large, fully double creamy-flesh blooms, deepening to rich pink in the centre and patterned with deep pink veins. If pruning is necessary, never do so other than immediately after flowering. It should be added that the great Gertrude Jekyll greatly approved of this rose, which proves us to be in good company. In case you are wondering about 'Blairii No.1', don't. It wasn't in the same class as this gorgeous creature. 'Coupe d'Hébé' also responds best to treatment as a pillar rose. Like 'Blairii No.2', it is essentially summer-flowering only and bears clusters of semi-double

pink roses on slender green canes. The foliage is light green.

It is entirely probable that the rose which is most sought after and asked for, most admired, most sniffed and most likely to cause symptoms of dementia in our gardens is the climbing form of 'Souvenir de la Malmaison'. It was called 'Queen of Beauty and Fragrance'. It was and is the best advertisement for the Bourbons. The huge creamy pink very double quartered blooms almost drip with delectable sweet fragrance distilled from the old rose scent cinnamon and, amazingly, ripe bananas. The masses of roses are set against dark leathery leaves 'like waterlilies upon a dark pond'. For those who cannot find room for this most magnificent of old roses, a bush form is also available, a neat, strong and compact grower. In England, it is said that 'Souvenir de la Malmaison' is not as remontant as the bush form. The Australian climate makes nonsense of that claim. Here it is never without blooms even in deepest winter, and the displays in spring and autumn are stunning, the canes bursting into bud every 20 cm or so. As well, it is marvellously strong-growing and will easily reach 5–6 m.

'Gloire des Rosomanes' (1825) was as often loved and known as 'Ragged Robin'. The large red semi-double blooms are borne in small and large clusters and are fragrant. It seems to be very variable in height, possibly responding to different soils. On suitable soils it may readily be treated as a pillar rose.

Among the glories of the rose world must be the lusciously fragrant dark red rose climbers of this century. Many are already well past half a century old and, if not 'old-fashioned', are certainly old in commercial terms. Not too many roses survive a decade on the listings today. My favourite must still be the climbing form (1946) of 'Crimson Glory' (1935). The fragrance takes me immediately back to my childhood. It is a hedonist's delight to be drunk on great lungfuls of rich, rich Damask fragrance until you nearly swoon with delight and over-oxygenation. The blooms are magnificent and of darkest crimson red. This was the rose that established Wilhelm Kordes reputation as a great rose breeder. All over the world 'Crimson Glory' became the first favourite, winning prizes everywhere for the best rose and the best garden rose. For those who are interested in rose form, the blood of the great Hybrid Perpetual 'General Jacqueminot' run in its veins.

The climbing form of 'Étoile de Holland' (1919) was released in 1931 by M. Leenders of Tegelin. It is a rose to conjure with still. It originated from a cross between two great red Hybrid Teas of the day, the beautifully scented 'General Macarthur' and the very fragrant 'Hadley', and went on to become one of the most popular red roses of the 1920s and 1930s. The roses are shapely, deep, deep red with a heady rich fragrance. The climbing form smothers in these fragrant blooms in a magnificent spring blooming, repeating during the season and with an especially lovely display in autumn and on into winter. It will easily clear 6 m in height and is clean and healthy of foliage.

Climbing 'Chrysler Imperial' is becoming very difficult to locate these days but what a joy for those who do. The huge deep bright-crimson blooms have an incredibly rich fruity fragrance that puts it in a class of its own.

'Château de Clos Vougeot' (1908) is a beautiful recurrent-flowering climbing rose bearing old-fashioned flat roses of darkest red, almost black red, with a particularly sweet pure fragrance. It was bred by Joseph Pernet-Ducher and it is a rose of dreams, our dreams of darkest velvetiest, fragrant red roses.

'Souvenir de Claudius Denoyel' (1920) is a hybrid of 'Château de Clos Vougeot' and does credit to its parents, becoming a sheet of intensely sweetly fragrant bright crimson old-style blooms early in summer. It can be expected to repeat bloom during the season.

'Paul's Lemon Pillar' (1915) remains one of the great roses of all times. Raised by William Paul from a cross between two famous parents, the Hybrid Perpetual 'Frau Karl Druschki' and the glorious 'Maréchal Niel', it produces an overwhelming once-a-year crop of huge fragrant very double sumptuous blooms in a pure creamy pale lemon-white, with a touch of acid spring green in the luminous colour of the heart. There is no rose remotely like it, and it is without doubt one of the grandest roses ever bred in every respect.

'Souvenir de Madame Boullet', a Hybrid Tea, was introduced to the world in 1921 by Pernet-Ducher. She has large elegant double old gold flowers of beautiful form and tough green foliage. The climbing form adds to its elegance with arching stems and is both fragrant and recurrent.

Some lovely older pink climbing Hybrid Tea roses deserve mention, and each of these are still available, which attests to their staying powers and enduring appeal. The climbing sport of the great 'Madame Abel Chatenay' arose in 1917 from the bush rose of 1895 fame. It has exceedingly good breeding—if it were a horse, one would certainly have risked a flutter on it. 'Dr Grill' (Tea) × 'Victor Verdier' (Hybrid Tea) produced an exquisite flower, very full, with quilled petals of light pink, flushing in the centre and on the reverse, and a pure, refreshing, overwhelmingly delicious fragrance not to be found in any other rose.

Lovely blush-pink 'Ophelia' (1912), the creation of William Paul from an unknown mating, is one of those exquisite roses that evoke sighs of memory from older visitors to our gardens. Nothing quite like it has been bred before or since. The beautifully-scrolled buds open to pale pink blooms of perfect form and its sweet scent is legendary. The climbing form will grow to 7 m. 'Ophelia' produced many sports, among them 'Madame Butterfly' (1918). The climbing form was introduced in 1926. It shares all the loveliness of the parent, with long high pointed open double flowers of a tender pink shaded apricot, and is very fragrant.

'Madame Caroline Testout' was bred in 1890 from a classy cross, 'Madame de Tartas' × 'Lady Mary Fitzwilliam'. It was one of the great hallmark roses and had an immense influence on the direction that Hybrid Tea rose breeding was to take in the twentieth century. It is superbly vigorous and floriferous, climbing easily to embower the second storey windows of a home with clear silvery-pink beautifully-formed fragrant blooms. It repeat flowers with great generosity.

Much younger, but still past her fiftieth year, is an exquisite little Hybrid Tea rose released by McGredy in 1932. It is as perfect in form as 'Ophelia' but considerably smaller, of deep pink, and fragrant. Its name is 'Picture' and the climbing form of this posy rose was introduced in 1942. It will reach a comfortable 5 m and is recurrent flowering. One more exquisite little pink rose must be mentioned, the climbing form of 'Cecile Brunner', the 'Sweetheart Rose' (1881). The perfect miniature Hybrid Tea blooms open from scrolled buds and are one of the glories of spring. They are in a shade of pure pale pink and are very long lasting both on the climber and in little posies. It repeat flowers but never in the abundance that spring brings.

One last glorious rose must bring us to the end of this chapter, climbing 'Dame Edith Helen'. Dame Edith was released by A. Dickson and Son in

1926 when it won the Mrs Clay Challenge Vase for the best new scented rose in any one year. (The award was replaced by the Henry Edland Memorial Medal in 1966.) The climbing sport (1932) has huge double cupped blooms in glowing pink with a rich stunning fragrance. If you live in a distict with high continuous summer humidity, this is not the rose for you. Otherwise, it is one of the great roses of this century.

Fragrant Rose Cosmetics and Perfumes

The morning rose that untouched stands,
Armed with her briars, how sweetly smells!
But plucked and strained through ruder hands,
Her scent no longer with her dwells;
But scent and beauty both are gone,
And leaves fall from her one by one.

Sir Robert Ayton (1570–1638)

Beauty and roses have always walked together. This loveliest of all flowers has valuable time-honoured properties for preserving the skin, and for preventing and even removing wrinkles. Its gentle astringent properties have been used for cleansing the skin and as the kindest of acne and blackhead treatments. It finds use in soothing protective lipsalves, and in lotions to relieve the chapping and cracking of skin in winter, and sunburned skin in summer. The rose has been used as a perfume, a pomade, in soaps, talcs and all manner of deliciously fragrant additions to a lady's chamber.

The old roses are the ones thought to be most valuable for skin care and herbal use generally. Many of the old Damasks, Gallicas, Centifolias and Albas that are traditionally used are in flower for no more than two months of the year. To have a good supply of petals throughout the year it is necessary to grow, gather and dry your own petals. It is vital that these petals are gathered from roses that have grown untouched by poisonous sprays, otherwise in preparing these cosmetics you will be concentrating spray residues and applying them to your skin.

There is no need to sacrifice lovely buds just as they begin to open. Go over the bushes each sunny morning when the dew has dried and cut flowers that have been open for a day. Pull the petals off in a bunch and, while they are still together, trim off the white heels at the base with one quick snip of the scissors. Spread the petals out in thin layers out of the sun, and place in an airtight container as soon as they are crisp dry to the touch. The better the airflow and drier the conditions, the quicker will be the drying and the better the colour, fragrance, and herbal properties retained. Many of the old roses intensify their sweet pure fragrance after drying.

It is a good idea to keep a row of old roses specifically for their herbal use, so that you do not feel that you have robbed your garden at the peak of its beauty. Most of the herbal roses make excellent hedges and could be used to form an informal hedge to a kitchen garden, or as a massed planting in an old-fashioned picking garden. Taller varieties can make a very useful, and impenetrable, screen planting. For lower hedging, the traditional herbal rose, the 'Apothecary's Rose' is ideal. So too would be 'Rosa Mundi', 'Sissinghurst Castle', 'Gloire de France', 'Belle Isis', 'Belle de Crécy', 'Tuscany', 'Rose du Maître d'École', 'Marie Louise', 'Petite Lisette', 'Botzaris', and the very repeat-flowering old Portland roses 'Jacques Cartier', 'Rose du Roi', 'Compte de Chambord' and 'Portland Rose' itself.

For tall hedging, choose from 'Gloire de Guilan', 'The Rose of Kazanlik', 'Ispahan', 'Quatre Saisons', 'La Belle Sultane', 'Président de Sèze', 'Surpasse Tout', 'Great Maiden's Blush', 'Celeste', 'Old Cabbage Rose' and 'Fantin Latour'. None of these tough old roses needs spraying to do well, so please resist.

Cosmetics can be prepared during the rose season from fresh petals, and for the rest of the year from the dried petals stored from the sweet sunny days of early summer.

From mothers and grandmothers most of us have heard of glycerine and rosewater. It was an essential part of almost every beautiful woman's routine. It was kept as a very necessary healing and moisturising lotion for the hands in the days when women were likely to spend hours in soapy water in the course of a day's housework. Mix thoroughly in a screwcap bottle equal volumes of glycerine and rosewater. Shake together well before using.

Milk of roses is another gentle old-fashioned remedy easy to make in the kitchen. Mrs Beeton gave her version as follows:

Beat 2oz. of blanched almonds to a fine paste in a mortar, then add 12oz. rosewater gradually, so as to make an emulsion. Have ready 2 drachms of soap, 2 drachms each of white wax and oil of almonds and reduce to a liquid in a covered jar near the fire. Work the mixture gradually into the mortar with the emulsion; strain the whole through a fine muslin and add 1 drachm of oil of bergamot, 15 drops of oil of lavender, and 8 drops of attar of roses, which should previously have been mixed with 3oz. of rectified spirits.

All of which remains more than a slight mystery if you were born 'post-metric' or did not receive, as the writer did, training in pharmaceutical dispensing! You will be able to translate not only the above recipe but almost all old recipes once armed with the following information:

Solids measure:
2.2 lb = 1 kg = 1000 gm
1lb = a pound = 16 ounces = 16oz = 453.59 gm
1oz = 480 grains
60 grains = 1 drachm
1 scruple = 20 grains
1 grain = gr = 0.06 grams

Liquids measure:
Cong. = 1 gallon = 8 pints = 4.545 litres
1 pint = 20 fluid ounces = 20 fl.oz. = 568.3 ml
60 minums = 1 drachm
480 minums = 1 fl.oz.

Without too much effort and mathematics any old formula can be converted to metric from this table, including Mrs Beeton's recipe.

Some more modern recipes use almond oil rather than first grinding almonds.

Rose Cold Cream

8 fl.oz. rosewater soaked with 1 oz. dried rose
  petals for 3 days and strained
10 fl.oz. almond oil
1.5 oz. beeswax, finest quality
5 drops Oil of Rose (optional)

Grate the beeswax into the top half of a double boiler and add the almond oil. Heat until the wax is dissolved and then remove from the heat. Very slowly add the fortified rosewater, beating constantly all the time until the mixture is fully emulsified and has cooled. Now beat in the Oil of Rose a drop at a time.

Mrs Beeton's old recipe was favoured for the treatment of sunburn and that fatal deterrent to female attractiveness in days gone by, the dreaded freckle. The cold cream makes a very gentle make-up remover at night. It can be followed by icy cold homemade rosewater from the refrigerator as a deliciously fragrant gentle astringent and moisturiser which both attracts liquid back into the skin cells and tightens the skin. You could finish with Cream of Roses, a recipe of ancient origins. The rosewater and honey have moisturing properties, and the mixture of finest cold expressed olive oil and almond oil would do wonders for a dry or ageing skin. It was recommended to be applied as often as one liked.

Cream of Roses

2 oz. pure honey
½ oz. (cold first pressing) virgin olive oil
½ oz. almond oil
3 oz. rosewater
5 drops Oil of Rose

Place the rosewater and honey together in a blender. Turn on to top speed and add the mixed oils in a steady thin slow stream. It will turn to a creamy mayonnaise consistency. Store in the refrigerator and use over a week, remaking the following week so that one is always using a top potency cream.

Mrs Beeton's recipe was quite an elaborate one. If you would like something simpler but perfectly effective here it is.

Milk of Roses

250 gm blanched almonds
rosewater

Grind the almonds to a fine powder. Gradually add rosewater, mixing thoroughly, to a fine thin paste. Squeeze the mixture through 2–3 thicknesses of muslin cloth, bottle and store in the refrigerator.

Your own rosewater can be made easily. Commercial rosewater is made by mixing distilled rosewater with twice the volume of distilled water just before use. It can be used in this form in the preparation of cosmetics, and as a fragrant perfume. In parts of the East rosewater is sprinkled upon strangers as they enter a house as a welcoming gesture. Rosewater is used too in all kinds of confectionery, sweets, drinks, and condiments, as

well as in various herbal preparations. Here is a recipe for making your own rosewater when the old-fashioned roses are at their height of flowering.

Rosewater

Gather rose petals of old-fashioned roses when the dew has dried in the morning. Cut off the white heels to the petals while they are bunched together in your fingers after plucking. Put 450–500 gm petals in a mortar and grind to a paste. Leave to stand for 4–5 hours in the juices created by the petals.

Place the ground petals in a ceramic or glass bowl and add a further 450–500 gm of fresh rose petals. Leave these to infuse in the paste for one day. Transfer the contents of the bowl to a pyrex or enamelled pan and bring to the boil. Strain through several layers of muslin. Traditionally, the liquid is then distilled, but it can then be left in a covered glass jar to infuse in the warmth of the sun for a week to 10 days before use.

Rose vinegar is an old beauty aid that found several uses. It was used externally as a disinfecting lotion, particularly for pimples. It is made by the maceration process.

Rose Vinegar

1 litre cider vinegar (traditionally white or red wine vinegar was used)
2½ cups dried rose petals

Add the petals to the vinegar in a glass jar. Screw on a plastic or inert lid and stand in the sun for 2 to 3 weeks. Strain the contents of the jar. Allow to stand for one week, decant off the vinegar and bottle.

These botanical vinegars are used to restore the natural protective acid mantle to the skin, to refine the pores and cleanse the skin. Dilute the vinegar with bottled spring water (unless you have a pure source of water in the country) and splash on your face or body after cleansing. It is excellent for 'combination skin' or normal to slightly dry skin. (For dry skin substitute the same quantity of dried clover, melilot, orange blossom or elder flowers. For oily skins, substitute with lemon grass.) The diluted rose vinegar is a good final rinse for your hair after shampooing, too.

Rose petal lipsalve is used for sore and chapped lips caused by wind, cold, and sunburn. It is a good idea to store this, when not in use, in the refrigerator to prolong its life and activity.

Rose Lipsalve

250 gm pure lard
250 gm fresh rose petals

Warm the lard in the sun and, when it is softened, mix in the rose petals. Allow it to macerate in a cool dark place, covered with a clean cloth, for 7 days. Heat the lard on a very low flame until just liquid. Squeeze through a fine cloth. Throw away the petals, pour the salve into a jar, and label.

Rose perfume has always delighted the world. A simple oil of roses is easily made from fresh partly opened rosebuds and olive oil. Here is an old recipe that still works very well, and smells delicious as a product. I use a refined olive oil for this recipe. Virgin olive oil, that is so vital to good cooking, carries its own fragrance and is to be avoided for this purpose.

To Make Oyle of Roses

Take a pound of red Rose buds, beat them in a marble morter with a wooden pestle, then put them into an earthen pot, and pour upon them four pound of oyle of olives, letting them infuse the space of a month in the Sunne, or in the chimney corner stirring of them sometimes, then heat it, and press it and strain it, and put it into the same pot or other vessel to keep...

From *The Charitable Physitian* by Philbert Guibert Esq., & Physitian Regent in Paris, 1639

This 'oyle of roses' is a neutral base oil into which is released the highly concentrated fragrant oil found in the scent glands of rose petals. The 'oyle' is very fragrant but is a very much diluted form of the very concentrated oil inside the petals' microscopic oil glands.

The pure oil extracted from the glands is a very different matter indeed. It is known as 'attar' or 'otto' of roses and is, and always has been, worth about as much or more than gold. The pure substance is a pale yellow, semi-solid crystalline substance at normal temperatures. It is extracted principally from Damask roses, Centifolia roses and Tea roses. Three separate types of attar of roses are extracted from these groups, each with its own distinctive fragrance. Alba roses are sometimes extracted too. Enormous quantities of roses are

required to produce pure attar. It takes approximately 30 roses to produce a single exquisitely fragrant drop, and more than 60 000 roses are extracted to obtain a single ounce.

Persia was long the centre of the production of attar of roses. The story of the discovery of this fragrant substance is a romantic one. It is said that at the beginning of the seventeenth century when the Princess Nur-Jehan was to be married to the Emperor Jahangir, son of Akbar, he ordered that a canal encircling the entire palace be filled with rosewater. It was said that the essential oil of rose separated from the rosewater in the warmth of the sun, and as the bridal couple rowed upon this fragrant river of rosewater the princess dipped her hand into the oil and discovered its delicious fragrance. It is said that she named it in honour of her husband Atir Jahangir and was rewarded in turn with an exquisite pearl necklace.

The story may well be true but, alack, a man of science—the Arab doctor Avicenna—was known to be extracting rose oil by distillation in the tenth century. Commercial manufacture of attar in Persia began on a large scale in the first half of the seventeenth century. By the end of the century, Shiraz was not only exporting to neighbouring countries but also to Europe. The Turks too were very important producers of attar and it was they who introduced their methods of rose distillation into Bulgaria in the late nineteenth century. In this century Bulgaria has become the world's largest producer of attar. Approximately 10 000 acres around Kazanlik are devoted to the growing of old fragrant rose varieties. 'The Rose of Kazarlik' is a variety of Damask rose that originates from this district and is favoured for attar production.

Another famed twentieth century centre of production is the cicada-shrill chalky sunny hillsides of Grasse in Provence. Most of the attar produced there never leaves the country, being used in the French perfumery industry. *Rosa centifolia* is the favoured rose, but Alba, Damask and Gallica roses are used too. The flowers are harvested each morning in the first half of May as soon as the dew has dried, a fragrant flood of millions of roses.

It is possible to make your own intensely fragrant attar of roses.

Attar of Roses

Choose either a flat shallow glass or enamel pan or a deep earthenware jar with a wide mouth. Fill with freshly picked clean rose petals and pour over fresh pure water to cover them. Each day for 7 days set the jars in the sunlight. After a few days a yellow oily scum will be present on the surface of the water. Each evening use a cotton wool bud to take up the oil. Squeeze it into a small lightproof bottle which should be kept closed tightly. This is the rare pure attar of roses. It can be made into perfume or diluted with almond oil to make a rich fragrant massage oil.

Pot Pourri is a traditional way of preserving the fragrances of summer, not only through the coming months of winter but, in the case of moist pot pourri, for as much as fifty years. Dry pot pourri is meant to be seen and is gently colourful. It deserves pretty containers, such as old cut glass jars and crystal, to show it off. Looking for pretty, unusual containers for your pot pourri can make visits to second hand and antique shops even more fun than usual. Apothecary jars and old fashioned glass sweet jars are also useful finds. Keep the lid closed on your pot pourri until you want the fragrance to permeate the room. Dry pot pourri can be revitalised by the addition of a little brandy. Once it has more or less lost its fragrance, you will find the addition of an appropriate refresher oil will revive the fragrance for about three to six months.

Petals for pot pourri should be gathered from freshly opened flowers soon after the dew has dried. They should be spread thinly on newspaper or wire screening in a cool airy place without direct light but with good air flow. For dry pot pourri, petals and leaves should be crisp dry. For so-called moist pot pourri they should be 'leather dry', with much of the moisture content removed but with a leathery flexible feel rather than crispness. Leafy material such as thyme, marjoram and mint can be tied in small bunches and hung upside down to dry. Never hang them in large bunches as there is a tendency to ferment and discolour, if not actually mildew, inside the bunch. Lavender flowers are also dried by hanging upside down. Strip leaves and flowers from bunches when they reach the appropriate degree of dryness.

Fixatives are vital to pot pourri making as they capture and hold the fragrances. Always use solid fixatives in a dry pot pourri. The powdered kind permeates and coats all the ingredients with a cream coloured dust and also coats the inside of the container, obscuring what should be a pretty sight. Quite a few people who think they are allergic to the fragrance of pot pourri are actually reacting to substances like powdered orris root.

Essential oils add concentrated fragrance to the mixture. Never judge a recipe by its original fragrance. All pot pourris should be left tighty closed in a cool place to mellow for at least 4–6 weeks if a dry pot pourri, considerably longer if a moist pot pourri. Here are some recipes from the past that will capture the true and delicious fragrance of summer roses.

Old-Fashioned Brown Sugar Pot Pourri

This is an old recipe which is known to retain its fragrance for fifty years. Firstly prepare the bay salt. To 500 gm common (non-iodised salt), add ten (preferably fresh) bay leaves and pound in a mortar. Remove the remainder of the leaves when finished and the salt will have absorbed the pleasant fragrance of the bay. A number of the old recipes for moist *pot pourri* contain this ingredient.

Take 16 cupfulls of 'leather-dried' rose petals. Measure the amount of salt calculated to cover the rose petals in alternate layers and prepare an equal quantity of brown sugar mixed thoroughly with allspice, nutmeg, cinnamon, 30 gm orris root, and 125 gm gum benzoin. To the rose petals add whatever 'leather dried' fragrant flowers you have to hand together with semi-dried rose geranium leaves, lemon verbena and lemon geranium. Lemon or lime leaves are another suitable addition.

Alternate layers of the floral and leaf mixture with the bay salt and brown sugar mixture. Pour over a good wine glassful of brandy.

Mature as per the general instructions, stirring daily. When the mixture is fully matured place in its final containers.

Old Fashioned Rose Bowl

4 cups dried red rose petals
4 cups dried rose geranium leaves
1 stick cinnamon broken in tiny pieces
12 cloves (whole)
1 heaped tablespoon orris root chips
5 drops rose geranium oil
10 drops rose oil
rosebuds and pressed rose leaves

Mix the ingredients together thoroughly and store for 3–6 weeks in an air-tight container. Transfer the contents to their final containers placing the rose buds and rose leaves decoratively around the inner surface of the jar as you will fill it. A tiny spot of partly whipped eggwhite will hold them in place while you fill the bottle nearly to the top with the mixture.

Thousand Flower Pot Pourri

This is the perfect way to use that first delicious flood of fragrant flowers in spring.

Collect all the fragrant flower petals of the season: tea roses which should be the bulk of the mix; *Jasminum officinalis*, jonquils, orange and lemon blossoms and their shredded leaves, tuberosa, *Acacia* blossom, clove pinks, lily-of-the-valley, honeysuckle, lilac, wallflowers, French lavender (*L. dentata*), which is the one flowering in spring, freesias and others. Following the general principles described above, alternating the 'leather dry' petals and salt.

Once the initial ageing process is completed, the second round of ingredients can be added. These should include a good proportion of the following: eau-de-cologne mint, lemon verbena leaves, lemon balm leaves, sliced angelica root, peppermint, lemon-scented and rose-scented geraniums, bergamot leaves, ground clove-stuck orange peels, rosemary, lavender foliage, sweet marjoram. To prepare the orange-and-clove mixture, cut thin peelings from oranges, lemons too if you like, so that they have no white pith. Stud with cloves and dry in a very slow oven until hard and completely dried out. Place in a mortar and pound to a powder. (The fragrance is utterly delicious). The roots and leaves should all be dry before adding. Also add cinnamon, powdered orris root, allspice, gum benzoin, a jigger of brandy, oil of rose geranium and oil of neroli.

Allow the mixture to go through its second maturation, then place in its final containers.

Nibbling on Roses

So sweet was the savour of the roses and other flowers and
simples that sick persons, borne within the garden in a litter,
walked forth sound and well for having passed the night in so
lovely a place.

From *The Lay of the Little Bird*, 14th century

It is always possible to invite your favourite
roses to dinner by including them in the table
decorations. A half-opened bud beside each
setting is a lovely welcome to any guest. Tiny posies
of 'Cecile Brunner' or creamy-pink Alba roses
mixed with fragrant lavender-blue or creamy-white
sweet-peas, or sky-blue forget-me-nots, are charming and not so large as to obscure guests and inhibit
conversation. At a larger table and for a grander
event a centrepiece of old roses can set just the right
note for a dinner party. One of our friends who has
the right kind of dining room for such an event uses
a large white china swan vase to decorate the table
during the height of the old-fashioned rose season.
Its capacious shape holds a tumbling glory of fragrant old roses from creamy whites through every
nuance of pink to rose, dove grey and grape purple.
The effect is so utterly romantic that a gentle rosy
glow envelops each guest long before the wine has
even been served.

Such mood setting need by no means be the only
role of old-fashioned roses at the dinner table. In
more leisurely centuries, any number of rose-
flavoured delights were served, and while we may
have largely forgotten such pleasures, many parts of
the world have not. The fragrance and rosy colour
imparted to foods by rose petals, and the delicious
wild tang of rosehips, are enough to justify their
continued use in cookery, but both the petals and
hips had medicinal properties that made their use as
a food doubly desirable in the eyes of past generations.

Over the years we have gathered together very
nearly a hundred old recipes using either rose petals
or hips and it is difficult to know which few to
choose. Each of these has been handed down for
many generations.

The old-fashioned roses are by far the best for
these recipes. The petals are not tough like those of
modern roses, and their strong sweet fragrance
permeates the dish. Hips, too, are best gathered
from old-fashioned roses and wild roses. Among the
best hip roses are the Rugosas. The single varieties
such as 'Frau Dagmar Hastrup', 'Scabrosa',
'Rubra', 'Typica' and 'Delicata' and semi-double
'Schneezwerg' bear huge waxen red hips like
glowing apple pippins. The more double the
Rugosa, in general the less likely it is to form lots
of these hips. Many shrub and species roses provide
a glittering treasure of jewelled hips. 'Frühlingsmorgen', with its huge exquisite single pink blooms
which repeat flower mid-spring to autumn, produces large crimson-red hips in quantity. Others
that are excellent are the *R. moyesii* hybrid climbers,
R. rubrifolia, the Cinnamon rose, *R. macrantha*, the
eglantine (*R. eglanteria*) and *R. virginiana*.

For gastronomic delights with a medicinal
purpose, the ancient Apothecary's rose (*R. gallica
officianalis*) was the rose of choice. (The word
officianalis was used to refer to a plant officially in
use in a pharmacopaea.) It is also known as the
'Rose of Provins'. Provins is a town situated south-
east of Paris near Nancy, and from the 13th century
for almost 600 years, people streamed into it for all
manner of rose-based products including 'Syrup of
Dryed Roses', 'Electuary of Roses', 'Vinegar of
Roses', 'Conserve of Roses', 'Rose Wine', and
delicious rose sauce. From the vast surrounding
fields of roses, thousands of fragrant flowers also
found their way into rose-scented snuff, rose sweet
bags of linenware, rose-scented candles, rose sweet
waters and perfumes. It is said that this rose
travelled to France from the East with the crusaders
Thibaud de Champagne and Robert de Brie, so
that it also acquired the name in France of the
Champagne rose.

Both the fragrance and medicinal properties of
the Apothecary's rose are retained and even intensi-
fied when the petals are dried. Medicinally it has
astringent and tonic properties.

R. gallica officinalis was one of the great colonial roses, carried round the world by those who emigrated to America, Australia, New Zealand and South Africa from Europe. It suckers well to form a dense plant and a sharp spade can remove rooted suckers, so that it was easy for neighbours to share this lovely tough old rose, as well as its herbal uses. It is very fertile, and seed was also sown for hedges by colonists, as well accidentally by hip-eating birds.

There is a long history of medicinal use for this lovely rose. The Arab doctors praised it greatly and Avicenna claimed to have cured tuberculosis with rose jelly (azuccar). It was used commonly in the Middle Ages for this purpose and quite a few cases have been quoted over the centuries of cures brought about by honey of roses, rose conserve or rose jelly. It has been used too in the form of a tea or syrup for symptoms of colds, and for inflammation of the digestive tract. A strong infusion of rose syrup was used as a tonic. In France a romantic and, it is claimed, effective alleviation of the stiffness of rheumatism has occurred with the regular use of several handfuls of rose petals in a warm daily bath. One imagines that the psychological benefits alone of such a fragrant treatment would make it worthwhile. A decoction of roses has also been used for minor cuts and abrasions, and on compresses for strains. As in infusion (tea) it has been used for sore throats.

Rose hips too have long been treasured for their medicinal value. They contain a high level of Vitamin C and were once popular in rose hip syrup, jams, jellies, sauces and tarts. During World War II when Britain was cut off from Continental supplies of drugs, the women of Britain were asked to gather herbs from the countryside as well as seaweeds from the shore as a raw source of drugs. Along with approximately 750 tons of dried herbs such as dandelion root, elderflowers, hawthorn berries, yarrow, comfrey and belladonna, some 2000 tons of rose hips were gathered. Volunteer organisations such as the Women's Institutes, Girl Guides and Boy Scouts performed an incredible feat in doing this. To gather 750 tons of dried herbs it was necessary to pick approximately 6000 tons of fresh plants!

But it is absolutely unnecessary to develop a sore throat in order to taste the delights of your harvest of rose petals and hips. Of all the flower foods that have been handed down to us these rose recipes are among the most delicious.

Why not celebrate the height of the old-fashioned rose season with a rose dinner party? Fill the house with old roses, scatter around books and catalogues on old roses and old gardening books for browsers, put on some soft romantic music, drift your guests through the fragrant masses of old roses in your garden with a suitably rosy pre-dinner drink, and then as night closes in seat them to a sumptuous array of rose-fragrant dishes. One annual event of this kind, that we wouldn't miss by choice for the world, adds mountain mists to the intoxicating mixture and finishes with some of the most diabolic Super 8mm film ever shot of the great rose gardens of the world. The camera quivers with excitement alongside its owner and tears frantically in an ecstacy of excitement through literally miles of old roses at Sissinghurst *et al.*, leaving the audience caught between dying of laughter and gasping in rose-induced ecstacy. The mountain mist has taken on a decidedly rose tinge by the time we leave. Guests are asked to bring 'anything to do with old roses' to share around, and lots of fascinating but nameless old roses arrive in bottles of water in the hope of recognition by a fellow guest. Exciting finds from antiquarian bookshops, jars of rose conserve, rose-bead necklaces, home-made rose pot-pourri— all sorts of things accompany guests to the dinner party to give shared pleasure. Cuttings change hands eagerly at the end of the evening to provide a tangible memory of a wonderful night.

Here are a selection of wonderful recipes for morning teas through to dinner parties. Indulge!

Pickled Rosebuds

Perhaps this old recipe sounds strange, but after all capers are pickled flower buds too. Tiny pickled rosebuds were once served with seafoods like crab and lobster. They go well too with chicken.

Baby rosebuds showing a little colour
½ cup sugar
2 cups white wine vinegar
1 stick cinnamon
6 allspice

Boil together the sugar, vinegar, cinnamon and allpice to form a thin syrup. Wash the rosebuds and dry thoroughly. Pack the rosebuds into a jar and pour the boiling syrup over them, filling the jar to the top. Store for two to three weeks before serving. Make sure that the jar you use is either a preserving jar or one equipped with a plastic screwtop.

An old recipe for pickled rosebuds can be found in Murrell's *Two Books of Cookeries and Carving* (1650): 'Pick rosebuds and put them in an earthen pipkin, with white wine vinegar and sugar and so you may use cowslips, violets or rosemary flowers.'

Conserve of Red Roses

For those familiar with the delights of home-made rosella jam, this old cottage delight bears a curious resemblance. Both jams are tangy and fragrant with a special wild sweetness. Unlike making rosella jam, however, you will not end up with a thousand irritating hairlike bristles in your hands.

Use only dark red fragrant petals if you can, or at least use predominantly red petals. Cut off the white heels of the petals before using them.

3 cups of rose petals
½ cup water
1 tablespoon rose water
500 gm sugar
1½ tablespoons of lemon juice

Place the sugar and water together in the saucepan and boil to a syrup consistency. Add the lemon juice and rose petals and simmer together until well thickened almost to the consistency of a conserve. Add the rosewater and continue to simmer until it sets fairly firmly when a drop is placed on a cold dish.

Fill small jars with the jam. Use on hot scones fresh from the oven with whipped cream, and to sandwich together airy sponges.

Rose Custard

6 eggs
2 cups milk
½ carton whipping cream
1 cup sugar
1 teaspoon rose water
2 tablespoons finely chopped dark red petals of roses
1 pinch salt

Beat together all the ingredients except the rose petals. Fold in the rose petals. Pour into a baking dish and place the dish in a second larger baking dish filled one third with water. Bake at 180°C for approximately 50 minutes or until the centre feels firm to the finger touch. Cool and serve cold. This is a very creamy and delicately flavoured old-fashioned treat.

Rose Butter

This delicately flavoured fragrant butter is wonderful served on thin slices of freshly baked bread. Creamy pale unsalted Continental-style butter is good in this recipe.

Cut a 250 gm slab of butter lengthwise four times. Line a glass dish with a thick layer of fragrant rose petals. Place on it a slab of butter. Continue this sandwich of butter and rose petals, and when finished cover the whole with petals. Cover tightly in a glass lid or plastic wrap. Unless the weather is hot, allow the butter to stand at room temperature for one hour before refrigerating overnight.

On the following day remove all the petals from the butter and cream the butter before using it.

Rose Hip Tart

From a 1671 book, *The Art and Mystery of Cookery Approved by the Fifty-five Years Experience and Industry of Robert May*, comes the following recipe It works very well using a shortcrust pastry and the hips of either the eglantine rose or of Rugosa roses.

'Take hips, cut them and take out the seeds very clean, then wash them and season them with sugar, cinnamon and ginger, close the tart, bake it, scrape on sugar and serve it.'

And delicious it is too!

Rose Syllabub

Syllabubs with their froth of cream and delicate flavour have for centuries been a delight of English cooking. The favoured syllabub was one made with rich cream, white wine, lemon juice and its rind and sugar. This old-fashioned variation has the fragrance of the rose with the tangy sweet creaminess of the more traditional syllabub.

1 cup whipping cream
½ cup rose wine
juice of 1 lemon
finely grated rind of 1 lemon
1 teaspoon rosewater
1 handful dark red fragrant rose petals
80 gm castor sugar
crystallised rose petals

Combine all the ingredients except the cream and crystallised petals. Leave to soak for at least 12 hours or overnight. Strain off the juices. Whip the cream until it is stiff and holding peaks. Gently fold the cream through the juice. Spoon into glasses and chill well in the refrigerator. At the last moment before serving float the crystallised rose petals over the cream.

Rose Honey

This honey has a wonderful wild tang and fragrance to it. It is delicious on hot toast, with fresh scones or pikelets, and can be added to herb teas and used in fruit salads in place of sugar.

Approximately 500 gm red rose petals with the bitter-tasting white heels removed
6 cups boiling water
2.5 kg light honey such as clover honey or Patterson's curse (salvation Jane)
juice of one lemon

Place the rose petals in a large non-metal bowl and pour the boiling water over them. Allow to stand for 12 hours, then strain off the liquid. Place the liquid in a (preferably non-metallic) pan, add the juice of a lemon and the honey. Boil together gently until it reaches a thick syrupy consistency.

Rose Vinegar

2 litres red wine vinegar
5 handfuls of dried petals

Place the petals in a wide-mouth screw-top glass jar and add the vinegar. Put the cap on the bottle and leave out in the sunshine for 2 to 3 weeks. Strain through several layers of cloth, and bottle. A little added to water as a gargle for sore throats is said to be effective. It is also an old cure for headaches. Place some of the fragrant vinegar in a bowl so that a cloth may be wrung out in it at intervals and placed on the forehead. Rest out of the light while doing so.

Rosy Fruit Salad

Combine together seedless green sultana grapes, chunks of fresh pineapple, cubes of fresh mango, slices of fresh peaches, a can of lychees, and balls of honeydew, watermelon and rockmelon. Add the juice of two fresh limes. Allow the fruit salad to marinate in the following liquid in a covered bowl in the refrigerator: Combine half a bottle of champagne (for 6 servings) with two tablespoons of homemade red rose syrup. Before serving scatter over a handful of red rose petals.

Exotic Rose Lamb

1 kg cubed lamb
3 green apples, peeled, cored and chopped into cubes
¾ cup coconut milk
2½ tablespoons raisins
1½ tablespoons brown sugar
4 thin slices lemon with peel
2 cups beef stock
2½ tablespoons freshly made curry powder
¼ cup chopped walnuts
4 tablespoons shredded fragrant red rose petals
¼ cup sour cream
plain flour
5 tablespoons butter
2 onions finely sliced lengthwise

Add the butter to a hot pan and when it is foaming add the lamb dredged in flour and sauté, turning often until sealed and brown on the surface. Add the onions and apple, then as they turn translucent the curry powder. When the curry powder is cooked for a minute in the butter, add the stock, lemon slices, raisins and brown sugar. Allow to simmer very gently until tender for approximately 1 hour. Remove from the heat and stir in the rose petals, coconut milk and nuts. Stand for an hour or preferably refrigerate overnight to blend and mellow the flavours. Before serving, reheat thoroughly (but do not boil), stir through the sour cream, and serve with hot rice. Garnish with fresh whole red rose petals.

Rose Petal Fritters

1 tablespoon Kirsch
¾ cup beer
½ cup plain flour
salt
1 cup finely chopped fragrant rose petals
1 egg white

Blend the flour, salt and beer together and allow to stand for 3 hours. Mix the rose petals and Kirsch together separately. Gently mix the petals and liquor through the batter. Allow to stand a further 15–20 minutes. Stiffly beat the egg white and fold gently through the mixture. Cook spoonfuls in deep oil until puffed and golden. Lift out with a slotted spoon, drain on absorbent paper and serve sprinkled with rose sugar. (To make rose sugar, alternate layers of partially dried rose petals with white sugar in a glass bottle. Allow to stand for 1–2 weeks. Sieve out the petals.)

Candied Rose Petals

Use large fragrant red rose petals for this, Hybrid Perpetuals like 'Baron Giraud de l'Ain', 'Gloire de Ducher', 'Hugh Dickson', 'Souvenir du Docteur Jamain', or 'General Jacqueminot'. Some of the old fragrant red Hybrid Teas like 'Crimson Glory', 'Tassin', 'Oklahoma', 'Tatjana', 'Chrysler Imperial', 'Josephine Bruce' and 'Papa Meilland' are also wonderful when candied.

Lightly whip the white of an egg with a fork. Cut off the bitter tasting white heel of each petal and, using a camel hair brush, paint each side with egg white. Sift over both sides with castor sugar and shake off the surplus.

Place the rose petals on wire cake racks covered with wax paper and allow to dry thoroughly in the sun or in a warm dry airing cabinet. Store in an airtight tin in layers interleaved with kitchen paper.

Caring for Old-fashioned Roses

O Rose, thou art sick!
The invisible worm
That flies in the night,
In the howling storm,

Has found out thy bed
Of crimson joy,
And his dark secret love
Doth thy life destroy.

Let us say at the outset that if you did no more than plant most old-fashioned roses and water them during the establishment period, you should be able to come back to them in fifty or a hundred years time and, with the exception of natural disasters and hormone weed-killers, find them flourishing and flowering. This is not a myth or a Garden of Eden dream. If you doubt it go to old cemeteries where roses adorn graves over a century old. Damasks, Gallicas, Albas, Chinas, Teas, Portlands and Bourbons like 'Souvenir de la Malmaison' can be found as healthy big bushes covered in season with flowers of excellent quality. These bushes have never been sprayed with fungicides or insecticides and have never been pruned. Of course the wild species roses can survive equally well despite such neglect.

With acres of plantings ourselves we have neither the time nor the desire to fuss over our roses. They are naturally tough and expected to survive and flourish. All hypertensive feelings about growing old-fashioned roses should be dismissed from your mind if you do *nothing* but water them you will still have a garden well worth owning and showing.

Should you still be concerned that the intervention of we mortals is at all necessary to the moral welfare of the old roses, it is reassuring to know that rose bushes have been known to survive a thousand years or more. The oldest known living rose tree is one that grows against the wall of the great and ancient abbey of Hildesheim in Germany. The best authenticated story of its origin is that the Emperor Charlemagne planted the tree in the year 798 AD to honour the visit of the Caliph of Baghdad. But other stories persist.

The most quoted legend, dating to the same period, concerns King Louis I of France, known also as Louis the Pious. The forests of Hildesheim were famous for wild boar and, early in his reign, around 800 AD, Louis commanded a hunt in the forests to be followed by an open air Mass. Returning home, the priest realised that he had left the cross used in the Mass in the forest. He went back immediately, searching everywhere, until at last he found the cross suspended from a thorny branch of a rose tree. He reached up to bring it down but, time after time, it eluded his grasp. After many fruitless attempts to lift down the cross, he returned to the king and told him the story. Louis I and his court returned to the rose bush and, taking the extraordinary behaviour of the rose as a sign of heaven, Louis I commanded that a great cathedral should be built on the site without in any way hurting the rose bush.

An alternative story relates that the Emperor Ludwig of Germany became lost during a boar hunt. The forests of Hildesheim around 800 AD were populated with numbers of wild beasts and Ludwig feared for his life in the darkness. Taking out his crucifix he hung it on a thorn bush, prayed for divine protection, and, crawling into the bush for protection, covered himself with his cape. When he woke in the morning the thorn bush had turned into a rose bush, and he had survived the night to be found by his servants. Convinced that a miracle had saved him, the Emperor Ludwig commanded the construction of the now great abbey.

Regardless of the truth of these stories, authentic records of the rose's existence can be substantiated for a period of almost twelve centuries.

As a broad generalisation, with the usual exceptions to the rule, the more modern the breeding the more some care is called for. Lots of old Hybrid Perpetuals, for instance, still survive as neglected plantings around old homesteads, in cemeteries, and abandoned properties. They are still tough enough as a group to survive considerable neglect. With few exceptions though ('Frau Karl Druschki' and 'General Jacqueminot' for instance), they are considerably reduced in flower quality and size and may often fail to repeat bloom unless nourished and watered regularly.

Hybrid Teas are almost always a problem in *au natural* culture. Some varieties really are tough. 'Crimson Glory', for instance, flourishes untended in more than one place that I know of and has received no human assistance to do so in decades. But these varieties are the exception. Evidence of extensive dieback can be found on most untended old bushes of Hybrid Teas. As a generalisation, when you plant this class you make a commitment to a maintenance programme that minimises the impact of pests and disease and provides regular rejuvenation of the framework through pruning. We find them considerably less drought tolerant in general and, like their predecessors the Hybrid Perpetuals, in need of feeding with a substantial diet to give of their best. There are exceptions to the rule of course.

It should be admitted that the Polyanthas and Hybrid Polyanthas, mainly from the early twentieth century, are very tough. We have found plenty of old bushes on abandoned properties, beside old cottages, and used in cemetery plantings from the late nineteenth century and the first quarter of the twentieth century.

On the other hand, all plants respond to sympathetic knowledgeable care. Roses that survive and flower well untended can be unbelievably generous when taken under care. Many of the old Hybrid Perpetuals, for instance, do well enough and flower quite well at the onset of the rose season when left entirely to their own devices, but do not repeat flower. Given a richer diet and regular watering, they may go through many flushes of flowers before the winter closes in.

Of course it is nonsense to say that the old-fashioned roses never suffer from pests and diseases. Of course they do, but with few exceptions they suffer much less in our experience than the Hybrid Teas, the modern class which has formed in many people's minds the idea that roses are somewhat delicate creatures, needing to be enveloped in clouds of filthy poisonous gases in order to stagger on through life. Somewhat late in the development of this class, which is well over a century old, far more attention is now paid to health, vigour and disease resistance in breeding programmes, and the Hybrid Teas are by no means the temperamental group of roses they once were.

Many members of the older classes of roses are, in our experience, very much less prone to fungal attack and this may relate to the thickness of the cuticle on the leaf, to the rugose (wrinkled) surface of the leaf, or to the leathery texture, all of which can be inhibitory to fungal attack. The vigour of the old cultivars appears to be virtually unimpaired by temporary partial defoliation. The same cannot be said of more recent classes. Plants which are well nourished and watered, with good air movement around and through them, are even less affected.

Our own display gardens, which cover several acres, are managed completely organically. No sprays are ever used with the very occasional exception of those which are garlic or pyrethrum based. Regular feeding with manures and heavy natural mulches provides all the nutrition necessary, and the bushes are very healthy. We completely avoid a monocultural situation by using underplantings and between plantings of largely aromatic plants compatible with the period from which roses date. Various species and varieties of lavender, rosemary, sweet marjoram, bushy thymes of all varieties, oregano, golden marjoram, borage, basils of many kinds, mints (particularly eau-de-cologne mint), pink-flowered onion chives, and perennial savories, with their masses of heatherlike white bells form the backbone of this underplanting and do much in our experience to help minimise the effect of insect predation.

While such root competition is not necessarily to be recommended in growing the twentieth century cultivars, the old roses appear unaffected, and are all the more attractive for having such a softly focused mist of colour clothing their nether regions. Old fashioned perennials complete the planting schemes.

When all else fails the Rugosa group should be considered. We have always believed in using plant materials consistent with low maintenance. To us this does not mean a sea of turf, asphalt and occasional junipers. On the contrary it means jungles of tough, healthy, genetically strong plants, well fed and watered, but capable of surviving in the ecological niche where they are planted. Our own interest in old plants may be partly romantic and historic, but it is equally a practical one. With minimum time and hands available, and a very large garden by today's standards, we find the old colonial plants, the tough survivors, are the ones that reward us with the greatest bounty of flowers and fragrance for the least effort.

The most difficult of all growing situations are those within reach of seaspray, on sand and rock. Yet there is a class of roses that can cope with such situations. All the Rugosas will survive and at least do modestly well. The forms which do not have the small carnation-like flowers will triumph. The species grows naturally on dunes in spray drift and can withstand subzero temperatures. In northern Europe they are used everywhere in park, hedge and traffic divider plantings.

The fragrance of the Rugosa is sweet but often different from that of other roses, just as the Musk rose and the Tea rose vary from the old rose fragrance; but it is possible to grow very fragrant roses using the Rugosas alone. They repeat flower well and most varieties follow each flowering with a spectacular show of huge red waxen heps. Harbourside and seaside gardeners are not exempt from the world of roses if only they will acquaint themselves with this group. As if all this is not enough, the Rugosas are unbelievably trouble free, the foliage always superbly healthy and disease resistant, culminating in a glorious blaze of gold, russet, and red.

A strange mythology has enveloped the old roses. It is commonly imagined that they belong in soft English mists. Certainly they can survive such conditions. Many thrived on it. But it seems to be forgotten that the old Damasks, Gallicas and others came largely from the Middle East and Mediterranean countries. It is a never-ending source of amazement—and amusement—to us that so many growers of roses exclude the old roses from their plans because it is 'too hot' where they live. They quote top temperatures of 38°C with some awe. In the historic Hawkesbury Valley below us where many much older than century plantings survive, and many newer plantings of old-fashioned roses have been put in during the last decade or more, summer temperatures may stay around 45°C for several days at a time, not dropping at night below 38°C to 39°C. More drastic temperatures can be quoted very easily for areas of Australia where old roses still grow on untended, particularly in South

Australia and Western Australia. As in the arid heat of the Middle East, the old roses flourish and flower abundantly and fragrantly in the heat of Australia, South Africa and California.

Humidity though is a real problem. Blackspot is much favoured by warm humid coastal weather of the sub-tropics and, as one-time Queenslanders, we would hasten to recommend that plantings in such areas concentrate on the old Teas, Chinas, the tougher early Polyanthas, and that magnificent old climbing rose class, the Tea-Noisettes. None of these require the, at least moderate, winter rest that promotes blooming of older classes. When temperatures rarely drop below about 15°C, many roses are forced to spread their yearly ration of flowers meagerly over a long period. The Teas and others mentioned, with their superabundance of bud and flower, very repeat flowering habit, and heat tolerance, are an excellent choice. Many coastal Queensland gardens boast very old bushes of Tea roses, and cheery little Chinas and Polyanthas. Many coastal homesteads boasted massive climbing specimens of 'Maréchal Niel', 'William Allen Richardson', 'Solfaterre' and other Noisettes, as well as climbing Tea roses like 'Climbing White Maman Cochet'.

Others who feel largely excluded from growing the old roses are those who have tiny gardens or even balcony gardens. Yet of all the roses it is the old ones that supply their needs by far the best. Many small but tough little roses exist in the old classes. The China and Hybrid China classes for instance have many useful small bushes that flower their hearts out, including *R. chinensis semperflorens*, exquisite 'Hermosa' with cupped pink fragrant flowers, "Little White Pet", 'Mignonette' and 'Anna Maria de Montravel'.

The Polyantha and Polypom classes complement the Chinas to perfection. They are equally floriferous and charming and include such roses as 'Cecile Brunner', 'Perle d'Or' ('Yellow Cecile Brunner'), 'White Cecile Brunner', 'China Doll', 'The Fairy', 'Green Ice' (yes it is a Polyantha, not a Miniature), wonderful opalescent 'Baby Faurax', 'Baby Alberic', 'Echo' ('Baby Tausendschön'), 'Orléans Rose', and 'Katharina Zeimet'.

For medium-sized pots try lovely 'Frau Dagmar Hastrup' with her huge single pink flowers and pippin-like scarlet heps, 'Yesterday', a Polyantha with thimble-sized exquisite blooms of lilac, pink or rose like elfin embroidery, and lovely 'Nozomi', the cascading Japanese rose that looks like pale pink clematis. Although not old, 'Nozomi' fits in perfectly with old roses.

Large pots, say the size of half wine casks (which look splendid in the right setting), will comfortably accommodate and set off to advantage many Tea roses and Shrub roses. Where light is a problem in narrow inner city gardens the extra height gained by tub plantings can often allow many roses to grow well, and of course the sour compacted damp soils characteristic of many such gardens is no longer a problem, as soil mixes can be brought in specially formulated for your roses. The added height of such plantings also encourages a graceful cascading habit. Good choices include 'Carabella', 'Papa Gontier', 'Jacques Cartier', 'Sophie's Perpetual', 'Salet', 'François Dubrieul', 'Mrs Foley Hobbs', 'Ballerina', 'Penelope', 'Proud Titania', 'Escapade', 'Felicia', 'Moonlight' and 'Cornelia'.

Tiny gardens can gain extra dimensions by using vertical plantings of climbers on supports. The pillar roses come into their own here being modest climbers mainly to around 3 m or a little more. Among our favourites for this purpose are the old climbing Tea 'Sombrieul' with its refined exquisite creamy-white blooms, reminiscent of 'Souvenir de la Malmaison', and with one of the most delicious fragrances in the rose world; 'Paul's Lemon Pillar' with magnificent huge bowls of flowers more luminous moonlight white, with a touch of sulphur and primrose-green in the centre, than 'lemon'; the invaluable Australian-bred 'Titian'; exquisite single apricot-pink 'Meg'; 'Climbing Pinkie' (a Polyantha); the almost thornless 'Summer Snow'; Veilchenblau'; 'Blairii II' and 'Sea Foam'. With increasing interest in restoring old gardens, many Victoriana-style garden structures for such charming lower climbers are being made once again by specialists and lend an authentic touch of style to a garden restoration.

Pruning Old Roses

The main purpose of pruning modern roses is rejuvenation of the wood. Aged wood bears poorly and its removal forces rejuvenation of the framework and improves flower quality and quantity. The need for rejuvenation has arisen, it would seem, with modern highly-bred classes such as the Hybrid Tea. Clearly such a need was not built into the original genetic makeup of the rose. We personally confine pruning to some Hybrid Perpetuals and all Hybrid Teas and Floribundas. With the exception of pruning out branches broken by storm-winds, old twiggy material, and straying branches across pathways, or occasionally improving the balance of shape in a bush, we do not prune. The roses bloom magnificently, the bushes grow to their natural form and fullness, and we are entirely satisfied that, in treating the shrub and climbing roses with the same minimal care that other shrubs receive in our large gardens, there is no loss of quality or quantity of bloom, providing the plants are well nourished and watered.

However it is a fact that some people positively enjoy being endlessly busy in the garden. At the end of a full week they feel a restless urge to be out and conquering rather than soothing their souls in a comfortable tranquil garden. So here is a summary of pruning practices for old roses should you feel the need. The roses won't!

Summer Roses—Gallicas, Albas, Centifolias, Mosses and Damasks

With some exceptions these roses flower only once per year. Soon after flowering they put out quite short new growth which hardens off and forms the flowering wood for the following year. In the manner of any shrub such as lilacs, philadelphus, and camellias, they gradually form a dense thicket of stems and a substantial bush. Old canes die out in usually between five and ten years. These can be cut out at that stage to neaten up the bush.

From time to time new canes will emerge to build up the framework of the bush. These should not be pruned under any circumstances.

The general rule with this group then is to remove any dead wood in winter, then leave well alone. With an old, well built-up bush some gardeners will remove one or two of the oldest canes, but it is by no means necessary.

Bourbons

Many of the most popular Bourbons such as 'La Reine Victoria', 'Mme Pierre Oger' and 'Boule de

Neige' have a tall willowy growth habit when left to their own devices. I personally find this charming. The natural semi-weeping habit encourages bud-break along the entire stem and in spring and autumn they can be clothed the length of the long canes with roses. I prefer to cut out the oldest one or two canes each year on a mature bush. They develop somewhat twiggy side growth toward the bottom by their fourth year that spoils the willowy effect. The same long willowy canes allow many of the Bourbons to be used as pillar roses (low climbers), or to be 'pegged down'. Pegging down is not space efficient and is suited to larger formal gardens. The long flexible canes are bent down and tied at their tips to embedded wire loops or pegs in the ground. Each cane forms an arch and is tied at the extremity only a few inches above the ground. By spreading the canes evenly an octopus-like effect is achieved. Because there is a lack of apical dominance in each stem, almost every dormant bud breaks along the canes creating an incredible spectacle of flower in late spring and autumn. For the same reason, climbers are trained to horizontal canes to encourage maximum bud-break and flower.

Gardeners with less space may prefer to trim out canes as they reach the four-year mark and cut back by ⅓ to ½ on fully grown long canes. The result is a bush quite covered with roses. The flowers tend to be larger and finer but overall, of course, there are fewer of them.

Some Bourbons are quite low growing and compact by nature and these may be pruned, if you wish, to the Hybrid Tea model.

Hybrid Perpetuals may be treated in the same way as Bourbons, either training them as a pillar rose encouraging taller willowy growth, pegging down, or pruning back. The flowers on pruned plants tend to be larger and finer, but the habit often seems sadly lacking in grace.

Chinas and Teas

Teas and Chinas have a natural twiggy habit building up with time into substantial, dense bushes. Tea roses have the potential to become huge. I have seen century-old specimens completely covering the front of cottages, literally rose trees with trunks some 25 cm in diameter, reaching to the roof of the cottage. Pruning can keep Tea roses within normal bounds and I prune them wherever excessive size is liable to be a problem, for example overgrowing a path. Old twiggy growth is pruned out and framework stems are pruned back to ⅓ or ½ in late winter. No matter when you prune Teas, except in cold districts, you will be sacrificing loads of blossom. So clench your teeth and prune.

Such is the vigour of the old Teas that the spring flush produces massive new canes covered *tout à fait* with as many as a hundred buds and flowers. Very high winds in early spring can bend these still sappy canes if the bushes are open to the full power of the wind, in which case I prune quite hard over the summer months, cutting long stems of flowers often, in order to avoid heavy winter pruning. The Teas are the most forgiving creatures though, so there is nothing to worry about. Leave them entirely alone, or prune if you feel energetic. Either way they are magnificent.

Pests and Diseases

There are those who are unable to resist using sprays made from brightly coloured packets. But it is true that where soils are exhausted, or where the ecological balance has been disturbed, there may be a need for interim help with sprays to tip the balance in favour of the rose until growing conditions have been improved. Suburban gardens often need help as infections and pests easily move on from garden to garden.

Aphids are the commonest pest problem. Also called greenfly, these are soft succulent green or light brown tiny insects which build rapidly in spring to dense colonies which cluster around new shoots feeding on sap. They can spoil the appearance of new blooms and foliage when in high population numbers. A hard jet of water from the hose will dislodge colonies. They have a number of natural predators including ladybirds, lacewings and hoverflies.

We use garlic spray if aphids are multiplying rapidly in spring. It is very effective we find, with aphids. So effective that they are stopped in their tracks. The first time we used it, many years ago, we thought it had no effect—until we tapped a branch and whole colonies fell off never to stir again. To make your own, put several cloves in a blender, cover and blend at high speed. Filter the liquid (coffee filter paper or cotton wool will do), and add to it a small amount of liquid soap (not detergent!) to increase the wettability of the compound. We dilute 1 in 100. In a particularly vicious mood I add a fresh chili to the garlic. Commercial garlic sprays can be quite easily obtained these days if you would prefer not to make your own. Don't use this spray on chewing insects however. You will just end up with garlic-flavoured fat caterpillars. A pyrethrum spray is safe to use, too, and is sufficient to hold the balance of aphid population growth at a point where natural predators such as ladybirds can often 'mop up' much of the residual population.

Malathion will eliminate an infestation for a few weeks, or you can use the systemic sprays Metasystox or Rogor 40 which enter into the plants' tissues and act on sucking insects for from four to six weeks. Use great care when handling such chemicals.

Thrips may be no problem at all for several seasons, in such low numbers as to be out of sight and mind. Then a bad season and a warm wind will bring a plague of them looking like shiny slivers of black ebony in the petals of the flower. They prefer to associate with white or pale coloured blooms. They are difficult to control over a period of time as they are winged and will fly in unpredictably from another area, and equally unpredictably fly off again. I put this sort of plague along with a number of other unnecessary performances of nature into the 'hands of fate' category. It *will* go away, and I don't particularly wish to poison myself with unnecsary insect sprays in the meantime.

Two-spotted mites (red spider or spider mite) are equally easy to identify. It is in hot dry conditions they are most likely to be a pest. Check under leaves for signs of fine webbing and, if your eyesight is good, fat globular amber coloured insects with eggs of almost identical size. These are avid sap suckers and can cause mottling and then defoliation of your roses. You will gather by now that I find the fragrance of roses and the Garden of Eden concept which each of us holds in our hearts entirely incompatible with dripping poisons. I'm sure that you too will be glad to know that there is an alternative to spraying, a biological control involving the release of predator mites. A fellow academic and friend whose enthusiasm for dealing with these creatures is

legendary, entomologist Robert Spooner-Hart, is one of the pioneers of biological control methods in Australia. He has carried out a number of trials on various commercial crops around Sydney with remarkable success rates, and now makes the predatory mite available to any growers troubled with these problems through 'Hawkaid', c/- Hawkesbury Agricultural College, Richmond 2753. Sulphur dust under the leaves will help otherwise.

Equally cheering to one who began her career as a professional plant ecologist is the safe control of all caterpillar invasions of roses with Dipel.

The only other major widespread insect problem is scale, and a surprising number of gardeners do not recognise those white waxy exudates on older rose stems as insects. Scrape a 'blob of wax' off the stem and look underneath. You will find an insect covered with a very thick layer of wax. The commonest, and usually perfectly adequate method of control, is to spray with white oil (at recommended dilution, with a follow up six weeks or so later).

The commonest of all fungal problems is blackspot which is most in evidence in humid summer heat. Many of the old roses are relatively little attacked and shrug off the effects so easily and with such undiminished vigour that the use of sprays would be absurd, like taking a ten day course of antibiotics for a 24-hour virus! On the other hand, some Hybrid Perpetuals are seriously disfigured by it although, from my experience, rarely affected in vigour.

Hybrid Teas are frequently martyrs to black spot and unquestionably their vigour is affected. Blackspot fungal attack is probably the commonest cause of dieback, a symptom characterised by progressive downward death of a stem, sometimes partly or wholly arrested by a lateral bud growth. Cut well below the point of dieback, a slanted cut away from a big healthy stem bud and approximately one centimetre or a fraction less above it. A second defoliation within a month or two can spell the death of the stem or even of the plant. (Check also for poor drainage and too much watering which can also cause dieback.)

Because I dislike a garden in which I trip over frail and ailing damsels and wounded soldiers, all of which make me feel uncomfortable where I would hope to find pleasantness, I grow few Hybrid Teas. Those that I do grow are usually the toughest, and most fragrant, of their breed. Recommended sprays include Mancozeb and Thiram.

Powdery mildew is commonly, although not

always, a spring and autumn problem associated with heavy dew falls during cool nights, followed by fine days. White or grey patches appear on the young leaves, then the whole leaf becomes coated in a 'white powder', becomes twisted and distorted, and then dies. Many of the old roses, again, will shake off the effects or are resistant. But more modern classes should be attended to by spraying with wettable sulphur, or by using fungicides such as Benlate and the systemic Triforine.

Mildew is most often a problem where roses are competing heavily for space and light with overhanging shrubs, or are planted under eaves against house walls.

For the gardener who shares my thorough dislike of poisons and who would like a peaceful, beautiful garden in which a child may nibble harmlessly on its fruits, salads, and herbs and touch flowers and leaves without fear, there is only one solution. Choose the tough vigorous roses that have survived for generations with or without human assistance; choose roses suited to your conditions so that they are not impaired by environmental stresses they were not designed to cope with, feed them with slow release organic fertilisers such as self-rotting mulches and well-rotted manures that do not encourage soft sappy overeager growth; live with some blemishes—only in death can there be waxen perfection; and think your way through a programme that uses modern alternative technologies where possible, choosing the softest technology available to cope with the problem in hand. I honestly have nothing stronger than sulphur, pyrethrum and garlic spray in my arsenal to keep many hundreds of roses in our gardens in condition. They aren't perfect, and in late autumn black spot does appear attacking senescing leaves, but the growth rate is astonishing. With the exception of four 'inherited' roses around our old cottage, no rose has been planted for longer than ten years, few more than five to six years, yet many visitors assume they have been there for fifty years or more. The incredible bounty of roses that shower down our mountain gardens testify to the wonderful vigor and floriferousness of the old roses grown with love, understanding, and only the gentlest interference.

Index